Nathaniel Marshman Williams, Justin A Smith, Henry A Sawtelle

Commentary on the epistles of John

Nathaniel Marshman Williams, Justin A Smith, Henry A Sawtelle

Commentary on the epistles of John

ISBN/EAN: 9783337729196

Printed in Europe, USA, Canada, Australia, Japan

Cover: Foto ©Lupo / pixelio.de

More available books at **www.hansebooks.com**

COMMENTARY

ON THE

EPISTLES OF JOHN.

BY

HENRY A. SAWTELLE, D. D.

PHILADELPHIA:
AMERICAN BAPTIST PUBLICATION SOCIETY,
1420 Chestnut Street.

INTRODUCTION TO THE FIRST EPISTLE OF JOHN.

For the sake of giving as much space as possible for the commentary which follows, the Introduction will be made brief. And this is the less to be regretted because there is no part of the New Testament whose authorship, purpose, and destination, are better settled among Christian students. If there is more question as to the other two Epistles, the whole matter of debate lies within a very small compass. Besides, some of the questions, which might under other circumstances be treated here, are sufficiently answered in the Introduction to the Gospel of John.

I. ITS AUTHOR.

The reasons for supposing John the apostle to have been the author of the First Epistle are abundant and conclusive. Although the name of the author does not occur in the writing itself, yet it is found attached to the early manuscript copies, which is an external testimony of no small value. Besides, Polycarp, an immediate disciple of John, quotes language from the Epistle, which naturally suggests not only its genuineness, but its Johannean authorship. Eusebius says that Papias, also a hearer of John and a companion of Polycarp, made use of it. Irenæus cites the Epistle as the work of John. Clement of Alexandria repeatedly does the same. This authorship is likewise indorsed by Tertullian, Cyprian, Origen, Dionysius of Alexandria, Athanasius, and Eusebius. There is besides the witness of Muratori's fragment and of the Peschito. "After the time of Eusebius," says Alford, "general consent pronounced the same verdict. We must join with Lücke in saying that incontestably our Epistle must be numbered among those canonical books which are most strongly upheld by ecclesiastical tradition."

The internal evidence of this Epistle being the writing of John is also important. It has that deeply contemplative manner, that type of spiritual intuitiveness, that refulgence of the love principle, that combination of tenderness and severity, which one would sooner refer to John than to any other of the primitive Christian men whose personal character is brought to our knowledge in the gospels or in tradition. One cannot surrender himself to the deeper thought and spirit of the Epistle, or dwell meditatively upon the words and style, without a conviction coming like an inspiration that the author was one who had a wonderfully receptive and absorbing nature, and who had stood in a relation of some peculiar personal intimacy with Christ, so as to speak and think more exactly as he did than any other of his witnesses. And who of all the twelve fits into these conditions like John, the beloved disciple? Then there is the obvious and very marked similarity between the style of this Epistle and that of the gospel bearing the name of John, which we do not need to illustrate. If John was the author of the Fourth Gospel he was, beyond all doubt, the author of the Epistle.

II. DESTINATION.

Assuming that this writing is an epistle, or letter, and not a mere treatise, as its pronouns of the second person, its familiar epistolary style, and its elasticity of manner, sufficiently prove, we ask, "For whom was it prepared?" The immediate readers for whom it was intended must have been, in part at least, converts from heathenism, and persons with whose Christian history the writer had personal acquaintance. They must have been persons having already an advanced knowledge of doctrinal truth and a long experience in church life—persons situated where the gospel had been planted long enough to allow of a considerable development of positive heresies. There is evidently a philosophizing or Greek spirit in the society where the letter goes, if not on the part of the readers themselves. The letter seems designed, too, to reach not a single church, but the larger Christian constituency embraced in a circle of churches. These considerations, and others, lead us to think of the great body of Christians in the churches of Asia Minor, and to a certain extent those on the other side of the Ægean Sea, as the readers especially addressed. The letter was an encyclical epistle for the great circle of Christians, upon whom the writer looked out with personal interest and knowledge. All this agrees with the Ephesian residence of the Apostle John in the latter portion of his life. Augustine's idea that the letter was addressed particularly to the Parthians must have been a misapprehension, or others may have misunderstood him. The presence of the term in the writings of this Father is satisfactorily explained in several ways, without understanding it to limit the destination of the Epistle to a single church or locality. No other preceding or contemporary writer lends the slightest encouragement to such a view.

III. DATE.

When we have reached a conclusion as to the author and destination of the Epistle, it is easy to form a somewhat satisfactory opinion as to the time when it was composed. That it was written after the Gospel of John is generally conceded. Again and again it assumes, on the part of its readers, an acquaintance with the facts of the gospel narrative. In several instances it utters, in a condensed way, things already stated in fuller language in the Gospel. And as a rule, as Lücke says, the shorter and more concentrated expression of one and the same writer is the later. The Epistle was undoubtedly written in the last decade of the apostle's life, not earlier than A. D. 90. The assumed mature experience of the readers, the well-defined antichristian error already developed, the long-established personal relations between writer and readers, the indescribable tenderness that breathes in the letter, as of one far on in the school of Christ, together with the child-relation to the writer in which all the readers are placed, point almost certainly to the late period to which we have assigned the composition.

We leave questions of style, objects, contents, and deep inward connection, to be answered by the commentary itself.

THE FIRST EPISTLE OF JOHN.

CHAPTER I.

THAT which was from the beginning, which we have heard, which we have seen with our eyes, which we have looked upon, and our hands have handled, of the Word of life;

1 That which was from the beginning, that which we have heard, that which we have seen with our eyes, that which we beheld, and our hands handled

Ch. 1: 1-4. THE INCARNATION AND LIFE OF CHRIST AS A MEANS OF FELLOWSHIP AND JOY.

The language is somewhat involved, but this is very nearly its tenor. The apostle has so much to crowd into his opening sentence that he seems scarcely to know how to begin. He wants to utter the cardinal facts in regard to the person of Christ, his own sensible acquaintance with these facts, and their effective relation to the higher life of believers—all in one beat, as it were. It is the effort of a full vessel to empty itself by an insufficient outlet. No expression that Christ made was so involved, or could be. Not even inspired men could speak like him. In the verses before us, we see a deep and vivid experience attempting to put itself in sentences. The life in Christ has become life in John, and he wants to make such a declaration, such a testimony, of it as will lift up all his readers to the same plane of divine experience. He knows that in order to be successful in this object, he must at the same time guard his readers against any erroneous views of the person of Christ. Hence his emphasis and amplification of certain peculiar facts in Christ's original life and manifestation to the world.

1. **That which.** The thing, or substance, which he will declare. It is not merely a person, but a person as a life, fact, principle; a new power emerging in human history. Hence the writer begins with a neuter, instead of a masculine, pronoun, meaning that wonderful existence which includes so much, that source of life. **Which was from the beginning.** We understand this to mean, from eternity. The words, 'was with the Father,' in the following verse, compared with John 1: 2, confirms this conclusion; so also, indirectly, do other passages (as Micah 5: 2; John 8: 58; 17: 5; Col. 1: 17), which declare the pre-existence, or eternity, of the Son of God. Of course, John 1: 1 is the strongest warrant for our interpretation. [See Note on John 1: 1.—A. H.] The word rendered 'beginning' (ἀρχή) may mean the condition, or foundation, which lies back of all historical creation and existence (Rev. 3: 14), and from which they take their start. Prior to the existence of any created being or thing Christ was—'was,' not was becoming. With what holy reverence did John contemplate such a Being, who did not belong to the common category of men, however truly he became a man. **Which we have heard.** The writer speaks for himself and his fellow-apostles, the prime witnesses of the gospel. The statement brings forward the eternal Word to a point in time, when, clothed with humanity, or, rather, made flesh (John 1: 14), he uttered human speech which ordinary human ears could hear. A testimony to the reality of the incarnation. **Which we have seen with our eyes.** The added words, 'with our eyes,' intensify the seeing, while they show that it was not merely mental, but physical, with the natural eyesight. It was necessary for an apostle, as an original witness, to have seen Christ thus. (1 Cor. 9: 1.) A blind man could not be an apostle. **Which we have looked upon.** This is something more than to perceive with the eyes. It states that while the apostles saw Christ, they likewise gazed upon him. They examined him, contemplated him. Their eyes dwelt upon him. There was that in him which awakened rapt and admiring attention. The verb here used implies something remarkable in his person, and is expressly used with such a reference in John 1: 14, "And we *beheld* his glory." **And our hands have handled.** They had handled him, and thereby knew that he was not a mere vision or spirit, but had a real physical body, and therefore was a man. It is the strongest kind of testimony to the humanity of Jesus. No doubt John here refers particularly to his handling of the real body of our Lord after the resurrection from Joseph's

2 (For the life was manifested, and we have seen *it*, and bear witness, and show unto you that eternal life,

2 concerning the [1] Word of life (and the life was manifested, and we have seen and bare witness, and de-

1 Or, *word*.

tomb. The humanity which he possessed before, he still had when raised from the dead. Jesus, in fact, invited this kind of testing of his bodily state. For when risen, and standing in a room with his apostles, he said to them, as they wondered and seemed to doubt: "Behold my hands and my feet, that it is I myself; handle me and see; for a spirit hath not flesh and bones as ye see me have." (Luke 24: 39.) And he requested the doubting Thomas to thrust his hand into the wound of his side, made by the soldier's spear, to satisfy him of the reality of his body. [Notice that the last two verbs of the original are in the aorist tense, and the first two in the perfect tense. This may perhaps be due to the circumstance that the last two refer to a single act, and the first two to an oft-repeated experience.—A. H.] And will not the same evidences present themselves when we shall see him as he is in his heavenly glory? Will not the hands and feet still bear the marks and scars of the crucifixion? (Rev. 5: 6.) Will not the body still be one that can be handled —real man as well as very God? This intense statement of our Lord's humanity was intended, as nearly all allow, to correct a suspicion, rising in some Christian hearts, that Jesus was not truly human, but only seemed to be so—an error which subsequently took more definite shape in the sect known as the Docetae. But take away the humanity of Jesus, make of the incarnation a mere seeming, and the whole scheme of redemption for sinners is undermined; there is no atonement, no coming of Christ into conjunction with our natures, no mediatorship, no sympathizing priesthood. The incarnation is one of the foundations of the gospel. And "if the foundations be destroyed, what can the righteous do?" (Ps. 11: 3.) Nay, what can anxious sinners do? How important the fact that the Word was made flesh and dwelt among us! **Of the Word of life.** Respecting or pertaining to (περί) 'the word of life'—that is, the higher eternal nature of Christ, similarly conceived of and named in the opening of John's gospel. The expression is thrown in to make his readers certain of whom he is speaking. All the preceding statements, he says, pertain to him who, before he was heard, seen, gazed upon, or handled by men, existed under the name of the Word, and contained in himself absolute life. He was called the Word, because he was the expression, the utterance of God, "the brightness of his glory and the express image of his person." (Heb. 1: 3.) And, as such, he was the original fountain of life—not merely of existence, but of divine, spiritual life. Before the world was, the Word had in himself that same Holy Spirit which was subsequently imparted to his humanity, not by measure (John 3: 34), to be communicated thence to all his people. The adjunct, 'of life,' literally, *of the* (true) *life*, is a genitive of nature, or characteristic. The idea expressed has its counterpart in John 1: 4. The whole expression is definitive of the opening words, 'that which' (ὅ), or may depend on such understood words as, I speak, or I write. Ebrard says it is appositional, and paraphrases thus: "That which was from the beginning, that which we have heard, etc., we declare unto you; and thereby we declare unto you what concerns the Word of life."

2. For the life was manifested—literally, *And the life*, etc., the free Hebraic connective so common in the writings of John. The mention of the life of the Word in the preceding clause suggests to the author a fact about it in connection with the incarnation—a fact confirmatory and explanatory of what he had already said, and in truth belonging to the very matter of his message—and so it must go in at once, parenthetically, before it is forgotten. The life, belonging to the eternal Word, was manifested in a human body (John 1: 14), making possible the action and testimony of the senses before mentioned. The incarnation, bringing Christ's life within the reach of men, before implied, is now more explicitly stated, together with an important fact in the process. **And we have seen** [*it*]. The word supplied in brackets is not needed, as the object is expressed after the two following verbs—namely, that eternal life. So Lange, Lücke, Ebrard, and the Bible Union.

which was with the Father, and was manifested unto
us;)
3 That which we have seen and heard declare we
unto you, that ye also may have fellowship with us:

clare unto you the life, the eternal *life*, which was
3 with the Father and was manifested unto us); that
which we have seen and heard declare we unto you

This testimony is not to be understood as the mere repetition of a previous statement, but as a declaration that while the apostles had seen Christ's humanity, it was not a bodily nature only which they had seen, but a bodily nature embracing and expressing the true life of the Word. They discerned in him a humanity containing the fathomless spring of eternal life. As they looked on Jesus, they saw, as it were, beneath the surface, and felt a witness that the eternal life was identified with him. Seeing him, they saw that life. He was the life. (Col. 3: 4.) They who deeply see Jesus discern the divine life in him, as well as the human. Enlightened souls have this blessed perception. The apostles, having had this complete perception of Christ, and being thus prepared in their own knowledge, went forth to the people witnessing of him, and showing that he was the true eternal life now manifested as the source and hope of eternal life to all who received him. And this witness they bore not only to the impenitent, but over and over again to those who already believed, to feed their faith and increase still further their new life. They report what they have seen and experienced, and by this means the true life is communicated and multiplied in men. They who experience a personal knowledge of the incarnation and life of Christ, become reporters, witnesses, to others, and so the vital knowledge is spread. Thus our verse presents an outline of the divine method of evangelizing the world. Living witnesses, who know Christ themselves, declare their knowledge in the Church and to the world. What we know experimentally of Christ, the life, let us report and declare. How otherwise are those about us to know the truth? **That eternal life which was with the Father.** The eternal life here is not strictly the personal word, but the life that was eternally in him (see 5: 11), and identified with him; so identified that the same eternity, the same relation to the Father, may be predicated of it or him. This is that infinite life, the pleroma of the Word; never coming into existence, but always being; which as such, or being of such nature (ἥτις), was with the Father, bearing a personal relation towards (πρὸς) him in the Word. As the Word was thus with (πρὸς) God the Father in eternity (John 1: 1), so was the life which was afterwards manifested in the flesh. Such a life must be ultimate and absolute, the basis of all other life, and its manifestation is the highest phenomenon; and being found complete in Jesus, it marks him as the most exalted Being. It is this Being who, while man, has a life reaching back into eternity with the Father, whom the apostles were declaring. It is perhaps impossible to decide whether the name Father, as used here, was applied in view of an eternal relation of fatherhood in the Godhead, or in view merely of a relation (not distinction) begun in time, with the appearance of the God-man. The former conclusion is certainly the most natural impression, from the use of language in the present instance; and if valid, implies a certain sonship of the Word in eternity. John is surely speaking of God as he was in eternity; but it is possible that he does this under a name which was given in view of the incarnation.

3. That which we have seen and heard declare we unto you. The apostle resumes the matter of statement begun in the first verse; and in resuming, after a lengthy parenthesis, he naturally repeats an essential portion. 'That which' has precisely the same meaning as in the former verse. The order of the seeing and hearing is here reversed, to emphasize the seeing as the higher evidence, the higher ground of certainty. Lachmann, Tischendorf, and Tregelles correctly insert *also* (καὶ) before 'unto you'—*declare we also unto you*—that is, to you also who have not seen and heard, that you may know the manifested One as well as we may, have the facts that we have. As the object of 'declare' is Christ in his historical manifestation witnessed by the apostles, it must refer to much more than the act of writing the present Epistle. It means, no doubt, the announcing of the story of Christ by oral communication and the written gospels, together with (note the present, or continuous tense of the verb)

and truly our fellowship *is* with the Father, and with
his Son Jesus Christ.
4 And these things write we unto you, that your joy
may be full.

also, that ye also may have fellowship with us: yea,
and our fellowship is with the Father, and with his
4 Son Jesus Christ: and these things we write, that
[1] our joy may be made full.

1 Many ancient authorities read *your*.

any testimony rendered or repeated in the present letter. The declaring is not effected in one way, or by one apostle merely. Having received the true light, these apostles enlightened others. (Acts 4: 20.) Suppose they had kept the great, new knowledge to themselves, what would have been the fate of the gospel? Or suppose they had spoken without experimental and certain knowledge, what effect could they have had on men? The apostles, as such, needed something more than a spiritual knowledge of Christ; they needed that knowledge which came from seeing and handling the human body, and from being with him from the beginning. (John 15: 27.) What is necessary for the witnesses of Christ now is the true inward knowledge of him. The subject of testimony, whether from apostles or from us, is Christ incarnate, and the eternal life in him. That chief matter being repeatedly declared by many men in many ways, the elect shall be brought in, and the life of the Church more fully replenished. **That ye also may have fellowship with us.** 'That ye also,' who have not seen and heard, may have fellowship with us, and so enjoy all that we enjoy. Testimony shall bring to you all that sight has brought to us; and for this purpose we make it. 'Fellowship' with another is something more than union, however intimate; it is a sharing together with a common partnership or participation of certain possessions, gifts, or blessings. Those who are in fellowship are partakers in common of certain things. It has been supposed that Paul and John differ in their meaning of this word (κοινωνία). "John's sense is more inward, subjective, than than that of Paul." (Hackett.) It seems to us that the participation, or fellowship itself, as an act, is the same with both; its objects may somewhat differ in the writings of the two—with Paul, the means of life; with John, life itself. And Paul seems to emphasize the objects, whatever they are; while John appears to make prominent the common participation itself, and the intimate union it implies between those who thus partake. With the latter, the spiritual partnership is all important, the highest exaltation. **And truly our fellowship [is] with the Father, and with his Son Jesus Christ.** The 'with' (μετὰ) is repeated before each person, strongly suggesting a real distinction of the persons in the writer's view. It must mean the same as in the preceding sentence—namely, in company with. The sentence is added (καὶ) to define the height of that fellowship of the apostles to which the others addressed should be admitted. It is nothing less than a participation together with Father and Son in a common life. That the object or contents of the fellowship is life in the fullest sense, is not directly said, but the tenor of ver. 2 teaches it. And fellowship with Father and Son in one great life implies perfect union and exalted companionship with them. In his deep experience of the eternal life which was with the Father, and in the Son, John was not selfish. He desired the members of the churches to share it with him to the full. They were already supposed to be converted people; but they might attain a greater fullness of blessing. It was their privilege to be on the same plane of conscious spiritual life with the apostles themselves. And how shall they attain to this grand realization? Let them receive a fresh testimony of the truth John is declaring; believe in the completeness of Christ the life; welcome the eternal life that is in him; know that it is for them. Oh, the wonder of the uplifting through the life that was manifested! The New Testament teaches that the Father has his name primarily from his relation to his only-begotten Son, and secondarily, from his relation to those who are begotten in his likeness by the Holy Spirit.

4. And these things write we unto you. By 'these things' he means these foregoing things. Compare especially 2: 1; John 20: 31; 1 Tim. 3: 14, and Ellicott on this last passage. The expression, 'these things' (ταῦτα), is used two hundred and forty-five times in the New Testament, and always, with half a dozen exceptions, with reference to

5 This then is the message which we have heard of him, and declare unto you, that God is light, and in him is no darkness at all.

5 And this is the message which we have heard from
him, and announce unto you, that God is light, and
6 in him is no darkness at all. If we say that we

things preceding. The reader, coming to the word in our passage, naturally thinks of the great things just mentioned by the writer. The 'and,' introducing the statement, helps the impression. **That your joy may be full.** Fulfilled, filled up, made complete. The things just written, such as the eternity, the real humanity, the eternal life of Christ, the privelege of fellowship with apostles and Father and Son, and the testimony of these things from personal knowledge, being read and experienced, were fitted to produce supreme joy—joy, and not mere peace or happiness. A cardinal object of the ministry (2 Cor. 1: 24), and of the gospel doctrines, is to produce this joy in Christians. "The joy of the Lord is your strength." (Neh. 8: 10.) It is the earnest of heaven, the essence of Christianity. "These things have I spoken unto you," said Jesus, "that my joy might remain in you, and that your joy might be full." (John 15: 11.) "Ask and ye shall receive, that your joy may be full." (John 16: 24.) Union with Jesus in the life eternal causes in us the same joy that, like a glad stream, ever runs in his bosom. Said Augustine: "There is a joy which is not given to the ungodly, but to those who love thee for thine own sake, whose joy thou thyself art. And this is the happy life, to rejoice in thee, of thee, for thee; this is it, and there is no other. For they who think there is another, pursue some other, and not the true joy." ['*Our* joy' instead of '*your* joy' is perhaps the correct reading; for it is supported by the Sinaitic and Vatican manuscripts, the oldest known to critics, also by Codex L., the Syriac Version, one of the Egyptian versions, the Sahidic, and thirty cursive manuscripts. It is the more difficult reading—a copyist would be more likely to write "your" for "our" than to write "our" for "your"—and therefore probably correct. Nor is the thought unsuitable. The joy of a true apostle might well be perfected by the growing knowledge and sympathy of Christians for whom he was laboring in the gospel. (1 Thess. 3: 9; Phil. 4: 1.)—A. H.]

5-10. FELLOWSHIP WITH GOD IMPLIES PURIFICATION FROM SIN, BY THE ATONING BLOOD, AND PERSONAL CONFESSION.

In the preceding section, John has set forth forcibly the incarnation of Christ and his eternal life, the preaching of which is the means of bringing God's children into divine fellowship and full joy. And now, in this second section, to guard against any false view of the way into this high experience, he shows that it is not by ignoring or denying our sins, nor is it by profanely carrying them along with us; but it is by owning them as they are, and getting clear of them through the death of the Incarnate One. The sublime, joyful, fellowship contemplated by John is thus holy on both God's part and ours. There can be no union or company with a holy God except in a way of holiness.

5. **This then is the message.** Literally, according to the best edited text, *And* (to proceed with the epistle) *there is this message.* The reader has here John's order and words. The message is the compact proposition, basal to a scheme of salvation, and primal in all revelation, given in the last part of the verse. **Which we have heard of him.** Not *concerning* him, but *from* him. The sentence recalls the idea that Christ, having become incarnate, spoke to human ears, and John and other witnesses did hear him. The thought is involved that the Incarnate One spoke for God with authority and infallibility, making it all-important that men should hear and know what he said. **And declare unto you.** Take up (ἀνά) from Christ and announce, or report. The apostles were in the position of simple reporters from Christ. The necessity of this work of reporting or announcing the message of Christ to men is implied. Preaching to men is as necessary as that Christ should first come and originate the message. It is the line of communication between Christ who came and the ears of the world at large. **That God is light, and in him is no darkness at all.** This is the message, declared from Christ,—a message testifying primarily of God; a statement lying at the foundation of the plan of salvation, and introductory to the atonement-word in 2: 2. Christ came not to say that God, in mercy to men, could be indifferent to their sin or careless of the interests of right-

6 If we say that we have fellowship with him, and
walk in darkness, we lie, and do not the truth:
7 But if we walk in the light, as he is in the light,

have fellowship with him, and walk in the dark-
7 ness, we lie, and do not the truth: but if we walk
in the light as he is in the light, we have fellowship

eousness, but rather to declare his righteousness (Rom. 3: 26), and his mercy by a way of righteousness. The *locus classicus* of Rom. 3: 21-26 is an expansion of the statement of our verse. John is deeply doctrinal, not less than Paul. Let it be emphasized that the holiness of God lay at the foundation of Christ's mission. The gospel throughout, both as a system and an operation, is a voice saying that God is holy; hence that man must be holy to be with him. But it opens the way of becoming holy. God is light, morally, spiritually. Light is the one most expressive emblem of God, and was created to be such. See Ps. 27: 1; 36: 9; 1 Tim. 6: 16; Heb. 1: 3; Rev. 22: 5. It represents God's pervasiveness of being, his perfect luminousness of mind, and the bright gladness (Ps. 97: 11) of his life; but, more particularly, the perfect holiness of his moral nature. This is the special point in the mind of John, as the following verses prove. See light expressing righteousness in Ps. 37: 6. The apostle intensifies his statement by putting it also in the negative form. 'Darkness' is named, not as the symbol of ignorance, error, or misery merely, but more especially as the symbol of moral evil, sin. In God is no sin at all. Sin can have no part in him, either in a thought, or feeling, or deed, or in a way of fellowship or union with him. His nature repels all sin. He cannot countenance it, either in himself or in others. Let no man, therefore, present the gospel, let no sinner presume to come to him, in a way to compromise God's holiness or ignore moral guilt. If the passage does not purposely confute an incipient gnosticism, it guards theology against it.

6. If we say that we have fellowship with him, and walk in darkness, we lie, and do not the truth. 'If,' here with the subjunctive, presents a supposable condition, an "objective possibility." (Winer.) 'If *we* say'—that is, I, you, or any one else. How plainly the teaching of this verse follows from the doctrine of the divine character just before laid down! With what tremendous force it comes home to any whose unholy lives, coupled with professed fellowship with God, are saying, "God is not so holy, after all!" If we have fellowship with God in one life (see note on ver. 3), between us and him there is community of character, moral likeness, and sympathy; fellowship must be mutual. Hence, for us to profess fellowship with God, while yet unsaved, or uncleansed from sin, is in effect to say that God's character is on a level with ours, and that he can have part in our sin! How many there are who are practically belying the nature of God, by thinking to enjoy God's fellowship here and hereafter, without regeneration, without moral renovation through Christ! But what does the very nature of God require? Darkness cannot be in fellowship with light. To 'walk in darkness' is to live in sin; "action inward and outward, in whatever way we turn." (Bengel.) Some specific, cherished sin may be referred to, and still the general statement remain fearfully true. Literally, 'in the darkness'—namely, that previously mentioned (ver. 5), which is totally foreign to God, but in whose sphere, or world, a Christian professor may walk, and so in a character opposite to God's. The expression is often used in these times of a doubting, comfortless state of mind, the opposite of a state of Christian hope. But the argument John is so powerfully unfolding demands the interpretation already given. Saying one thing and denying it in act, we tell a lie in both word and deed. Doing not the truth is something more than the act of lying, expressed negatively; something more than acting inconsistently. It comes nearer to being the negative expression of walking in darkness. It is the failure to express the light of God's nature in our life, the failure to do the gospel truth as the tree *does* its fruit. (Matt. 3: 8, 10, in the Greek.) Truth here does not vary essentially from its Johannean meaning, and doing the truth is well explained in John 3: 21. "That the truth (τὴν ἀλήθειαν) can mean only the substantial truth, that which in its nature is conformed to the nature of the God of light, ought never to be doubted." (Ebrard.)

7. But if we walk in the light, as he is in the light. If God is light, it is likewise the element in which he lives. It encircles

we have fellowship one with another, and the blood of Jesus Christ his Son cleanseth us from all sin.

one with another, and the blood of Jesus his Son
8 cleanseth us from all sin. If we say that we have

every part and point of his being. In the same sphere or state of moral light we may walk—that is, in moral harmony with God, which is righteousness; and if we do, it implies and proves two things. **We have fellowship one with another.** Saying that we have this fellowship does not prove that we are walking in the light; but walking in the light proves that we have this fellowship. Where there is the former, expect to find the latter. Who are the parties included in the phrase 'one with another'—Christians only, or Christians and God himself? We should say the latter. John is certainly arguing about a fellowship that includes God, and the walk that evinces it or denies it. Besides, the pronoun *his* in the next part of the verse most naturally supposes that the idea of God is not dropped from the present part. Nor does this view, as some aver (see Lange), put God and us too nearly on a level; since it belongs to the very idea of fellowship, as between God and us, that he permits himself to be on a kind of level with us. Wonderful permission and admission! Nor, in fact, is God brought down in the reality of this community, but the sinner rather in Christ is lifted up into the life of God. On the plane of this high fellowship of God and his people, each participates with each, and each with all, in the fullest mutuality—one with another (μετ' ἀλλήλων). **And the blood of Jesus Christ his Son cleanseth us from all sin.** The best supported text omits the term 'Christ.' John meets a mental question, Have these Christians, up in this high state, no sins? Yes, says John in effect, they have sins, but the blood of Jesus cleanses them all away, so that, consciously forgiven, saved, washed, they walk in God's light; and this walking involves and proves the cleansing, as it did the fellowship. The cleansing and fellowship, too, are most intimately connected. The consciousness of the one involves that of the other; and there is no fellowship without cleansing. The blood is the atoning or sacrificial work, through faith in which (Acts 15: 9) we are cleansed from sin. Being the blood of the Son of God, it is of infinite value in canceling penalty. 'Cleanseth us from all sin' should be translated *is cleansing us from every sin.* Their importance, as bearing upon certain modern opinions, cannot be overestimated. Do they describe a work of sanctification, or of justification? Our answer is, a work of justification. A statement directly parallel we find in Rom. 5: 9, "Being now justified by his blood." The blood justifies, while it is the Spirit which sanctifies. These separate offices should be carefully distinguished. To justify a person from a sin is to free him from it, so that it is no longer his. It is more than to pardon the person; it is to take away his guilt, so that the sin is no more chargeable to him. He stands as one innocent before the divine law. Condemnation is gone from the conscience; and with it departs the sense of moral pollution. Now, does not *cleansing us* well describe this total act which frees us from the sin, utterly disengages us from it, so that it is no more ours? And is not this just the work of cleansing that is described in Heb 9: 14, and is there, as in our passage, referred to 'the blood of Christ? Compare, also, Heb. 1: 3; 9: 22; 2 Peter 1: 9, and especially the analogy of Lev. 16: 19, 20. The act of the cleansing is present and continuous (καθαρίζει), and is such at all parts of the Christian life on earth, implying that at every successive moment there is accruing sin. The continuous, erasive work of the atonement implies that there is constantly recurring sin to be erased. No sin, no cleansing. But there is cleansing, and therefore sin. At this moment, looking at the blood of Christ, I realize that I am fully cleansed, justified; but, having the remains of the old nature, sin accrues, and I need to make a constantly fresh application of his blood; and making it for one moment or many, I am conscious of complete cleansing from guilt, of full salvation. The full salvation, however continuously realized, is not a state of sinlessness. The sin constantly flows in, the irruption ceases not, but the blood of Christ meets it and cleanses us from it, giving constant victory to constant appropriating faith. The passage teaches this seeming but easily comprehended paradox, that at each moment we need salvation from sin, and at each moment we may realize full cleansing. Finally, observe that the work being done by

8 If we say that we have no sin, we deceive ourselves, and the truth is not in us.

9 If we confess our sins, he is faithful and just to forgive us *our* sins, and to cleanse us from all unrighteousness.

10 If we say that we have not sinned, we make him a liar, and his word is not in us.

no sin, we deceive ourselves, and the truth is not in
9 us. If we confess our sins, he is faithful and righteous to forgive us our sins, and to cleanse us from
10 all unrighteousness. If we say that we have not
sinned, we make him a liar, and his word is not in
us.

the appropriated blood is not the taking away of the root principle of sin, but rather of each particular sin, *every sin.* The old root, whence the sin comes, is not removed by the blood; that can be met or in any measure subdued only by the Spirit. It is the guilt of sin, not the sinning nature, which the blood removes. The sinning nature may be likened to an old sore, whose continuous eruption the "fuller's soap" cleanses away, while itself remains. What Paul had the battle with was not unforgiven sin, but the sinning nature, which as a deep sore he felt to be active within him. But while feeling the grievous motions of sin, it was his privilege to feel the constant cleansing of the Saviour's blood, and so a happy victory, of which he testifies, and delightful fellowship with God.

8. If we say that we have no sin, we deceive ourselves. John includes himself in this statement. If after any of us are once saved and cleansed by the blood of Christ, we say we have no accruing sin needing atonement, we deceive ourselves. If the ripest Christian says he has not an active sinning nature hidden as a root within him, from which guilt and pollution will arise, needing the cleansing blood of Jesus, that man does not know himself; he is deluded. **And the truth is not in us.** The truth here is the truth of the gospel, bringing the light of God into the soul, and so revealing sins as the sunlight does the dust. See Ps. 90: 8. "The truth is to be taken objectively as the divine truth in Christ, the absolute principle of life from God received into the heart" (Lange); "the objective essence of the divine nature, which is light" (Ebrard); "true faith" (Fausset); "the truth respecting God's holiness and our sinfulness, which is the very first spark of light in us" (Alford).

9. If we confess our sins. Our method of obtaining the full effect of the cleansing blood. It is by confessing our sins (not our mere sinfulness), voluntarily uncovering them before the eye of God, which is essentially repentance. See Ps. 32: 5, 6. Such repentance is not without an element of faith; and the result follows—full salvation. **He is faithful and just.** He—namely, God. 'Faithful' to his promise of forgiveness upon condition of repentance, and just inasmuch as Christ has died for our sins. (Rom. 3: 26.) **To forgive us our** (literally, *the*) **sins, and to cleanse us from all** (literally, *every*) **unrighteousness.** 'He is faithful and just'—*righteous*—for this very purpose, to this very end (ἵνα), that he should not only forgive the confessed sins, but, what is more, take away the guilt, free us from the sins, justify us, so that we stand as innocent before him. See note on ver. 7.

10. If we say that we have not sinned. The persons supposed to say this are viewed at the point when they should be offering their confession—a confession of sins beginning in the past and reaching down to the present; hence, the perfect tense. But if when they should begin to confess the sins of the time covered by this tense down to the present moment, they say, 'We have not sinned,' there is a terrible added sin. **We make him a liar.** That is, God. "We not only lie (ver. 6), and are deluded (ver. 8), but even more than that, we make God a liar. For he has said by others, and just now by me (John), that we all have ever-recurring sins." **And his word is not in us.** (John 5: 38.) His word of the gospel, as a living principle (1 Peter 1: 23), the seed of the new nature. It corresponds substantially with the truth in ver. 8, and confirms the interpretation there given. Implanted in us by the Spirit, it reveals to us our sins, and our constant need of the atoning blood.

CHAPTER II.

MY little children, these things write I unto you, that ye sin not. And if any man sin, we have an advocate with the Father, Jesus Christ the righteous:

1 My little children, these things I write unto you, that ye may not sin. And if any man sin, we have

Ch. 2: 1, 2. THE WRITER'S OBJECT IS TO PREVENT SIN IN BELIEVERS; BUT HE WOULD ALSO SAVE THEM FROM DESPAIR IN CASE THEY DO SIN.

Notwithstanding the clearness of the words and style, it is by no means easy to summarize the thought of these verses. There is evidently a very close connection between them and the verses immediately preceding; and a remembrance of this will aid the interpretation.

1. My little children. The aged apostle, great in gentleness, so calls the Christians whom he addresses. He may have been led to the use of these words by many reasons: 1. Because he was a very old man, by whom even middle-aged people would be thought of as young. 2. Because he was conscious of a fatherly care and love for the disciples of Christ. 3. Because he had been instrumental in the conversion, or rather regeneration (τεκνία), of many of those to whom he wrote. Paul uses the same words for this reason in Gal. 4: 19; compare 1 Cor. 4: 15. 4. Because they possessed a humble, simple, childlike nature, after conversion (see Matt. 18: 3, 4, 5, 6, 10), which drew them to him as their spiritual guide and overseer. 5. Because in their present imperfect and dependent state, they needed to be led by further instruction into the light of doctrine and life. The term 'little' is undoubtedly expressive of endearment. And John uses the whole phrase in the most eager affectionate solicitude for the welfare of the persons to whom it applies. The phrase itself is a loving appeal and protecting assurance. **These things write I unto you, that ye sin not.** One might connect this very closely, and almost exclusively, with the last verse of the preceding chapter, and say: "That ye sin *not*"—the sin just spoken of; to wit, that of making God a liar. But beyond question our verse has a broader connection, through the expression 'these things' (ταῦτα), with the preceding chapter; and the sin sought to be prevented is more general. John had just told how men come into conscious fellowship with God. It is not by ignoring their sins, but by recognizing and confessing them, and then feeling that the blood of Jesus has cleansed away all guilt. Freed in this gospel manner from all unrighteousness, they come into holy light, and have fellowship with God. Now it is this comprehensive matter which John says he writes, that his readers sin not. And what he had thus said would tend to produce this effect. 1. Because it pointed out to them their faults and their liability to sin. This of itself would put them on their guard against sinning. 2. Because it inculcated the duty of confession, and where one is under a law to uncover his sins it makes him more careful about contracting sins which he must thus uncover and confess. 3. Because if they should thus come into the blessed sense of complete cleansing, or justification, through the blood of Christ, that very state of conscious cleansing would be the best possible preservative against subsequent sins. The consciousness of being justified from past sins is the best foundation of holy living afterwards. In fact, there is no evangelical holiness which does not spring from a sense of justification. If, therefore, says John, I can get you, through humble confession, to feel the perfect cleansing of the atoning blood, I lay the basis of a holy life in you. The remaining old nature in you is a sinning nature, but you will sin the less, you will more and more overcome, when once you feel justified. What John says is a suggestive statement of the truth, that a holy life, a sin-conquering life, can only come from a sense of pardon; that progressive sanctification is from the fountain of an ever newly realized justification. **And if any man** (ἐάν τις) **sin, we have,** etc. The term 'we' shows that the supposed case is within the Christian ranks. It is sin after one is forgiven that is supposed, and for which provision in the gospel is expressly asserted. It is as if John had said: "The aim of the gospel, as a ready means of cleansing, is not to encourage but to prevent sinning—that ye may not sin; and (καί) still do not be cast down if sin transpires; for while

2 And he is the propitiation for our sins: and not
for ours only, but also for *the sins of* the whole world.

an [1] Advocate with the Father, Jesus Christ the
2 righteous: and he is the propitiation for our sins;

[1] Or, *Comforter; or, Helper.* Gr. *Paraclete.*

holiness is your aim, though there may be failures, Christ is your friend, and he will stand for you. It is a word of animation for those who feel the holy design of the gospel and are striving to realize it, while they are painfully conscious of remaining sin. **An advocate with the Father, Jesus Christ the** (better, *who is*) **righteous.** The adjective has no article, and is simply predicative. The whole expression declares a fact and doctrine most wonderful, most comforting. But only Christians can claim the fact for themselves. Christ is the Advocate of his people only. 'We have,' etc. It was so in chapter 17 of the Gospel of John; it is so in heaven to-day; it will be so at the judgment day. God the Father is light, and in him there is no darkness at all. The least sin is an infinite evil, and an infinite offense against God's nature. A sin, by whomsoever committed, has a germ of hell in it. If the work of Christ did not continue to avail for men after their conversion, their sins would consign them again to perdition, through the necessary action of divine justice. Christians need effectual advocacy to shield them after they are converted. The word 'advocate,' or *paraclete*, here used is the same which is applied to the Holy Spirit in John 14: 16, 26; 15: 26; 16: 7, and is there rendered "Comforter." In John 14: 16, the name is impliedly given to Christ as well. It belongs to one who is called to the side, or help, of another (παρά and καλέω). Obviously it fitly names the leading office of the Spirit or of Christ. Applied to the Spirit, it designates him comprehensively as our Helper, inasmuch as he takes of the things of Christ and shows them unto us, and as he becomes an *intercessor in us.* (Rom. 8: 26.) [Christ is our Advocate with the Father, the Holy Spirit is Christ's Advocate with us.—A. H.] Applied to Christ, it designates him as our Helper; but whose help is chiefly, and wholly so in our passage, as an intercessor, pleader, proxy, advocate, *for us, in heaven.* (Rom. 8: 34; Heb. 7: 25.) Christ stands for us as his clients in the court of heaven. He is there with his atonement, and all helpful appeal and defense, on the basis of it. A priestly advocate (ver. 2), and he will clear us. We have a living Saviour, who though ascended is still working for his people. The advocacy is successful, because it is that of Jesus Christ, and of him 'righteous.' Being completely righteous, he could atone for others; loving righteousness, he would vindicate divine justice while pleading the cause of the penitent; having a righteous sense of the sinfulness of sin and its eternal judgment, he would feel the weight of the matter, and rather die than see justice sacrificed. And if he pleads, it is not on the lightness of the offense or for sentimental mercy, but with the argument of the punishment endured in himself. In all his work for sinners, Christ, being righteous, studies the interests of righteousness, and identifies himself with the cause of righteousness, and so the Father regards the advocate's plea. The advocate is on the side of the law.

2. And he is the (rather, *a*) **propitiation for our sins.** What the word 'righteous' (δίκαιον) somewhat anticipated, what is necessary to the plea of the Righteous One, is now expressly unfolded. The advocate is himself (αὐτός) the satisfaction of the sinner's penalty. What a warrant this gives the pleader! Christ did not accomplish the propitiation as a mere act, but he was, as Ebrard says, with his whole being and life a personal propitiation; and the propitiation is still a reality, forever continuing its effect in his person. As Lange says, it is of perpetual validity and operation (ἐστί). He who is a propitiator through himself is propitiation. That word has a great part of the theology of salvation in it. It is of God's eternal nature to be just. That is a fundamental proposition, standing as a base of granite beneath the whole gospel superstructure. Everything must be worked out in accord with that proposition. God is just towards sin. His nature burns with holy wrath against it. He judges it. Were it otherwise, he would not be God. And this judgment is not accidental, not contingent, but necessary and unchangeable. Now the Son of God knew this, and was in cordial, infinite sympathy with it. But was there any

3 And hereby we do know that we know him, if we keep his commandments.

and not for ours only, but also for the whole world.
3 And hereby know we that we know him, if we keep

way by which a penitent sinner might be saved from this eternal judgment? Yes; by the Son of God taking the sinner's place, and suffering the judgment belonging to the sinner. So he stood as a sinner, "made sin," and received the shafts of eternal judgment. It was satisfaction of divine justice. The divine propitiousness ensues. Thus the mercy of God towards any sinner is not mere mercy, but propitiated mercy, a mercy that regards justice. This is the mercy the publican cried for. (Luke 18: 13.) Be propitious to me, he said. The entire principle is powerfully set forth in Rom. 3: 23-26. See 1 John 4: 10; Heb. 2: 17. **And not for ours only, but also for the sins of the whole world.** The whole moral world, impliedly a sinning world, considered as needing propitiation in its relation to God. The expression 'for the whole world' is a condensation of '*for the sins of the whole world*,' as the previous clause and the very meaning of the propitiation show. A brevil-oquence, Ebrard calls it, and compares John 5: 36; an *oratio variata*, Winer says, and refers to Heb. 9: 7 and Acts 20: 26. Christ is the Paraclete of his people, but the propitiation of men in general. The statement is designed to set forth the sufficiency of the atonement for any number of sins or sinners, and so relieve his readers from all fear that they might exhaust the provision before they had got rid of all their sins. John says it is sufficient in itself for each of their thousand sins (note the plural) and for each one of the numberless sins of every sinful man on earth in all time. Compare John 1: 29, where the general doctrine is similar, but the term for sin is in the singular number and collective sense. The condition of the atonement becoming effectually ours had been stated in the preceding chapter, and did not require repetition. This condition had been stated to be repentance, including confession, implying indeed faith. (1: 9.) Paul also declares that the propitiation is through faith in his blood, or made available thereby, and is wrought, in order that God might justify him that believeth. (Rom. 3: 25, 26.) The propitiation is for our sins as often as we will confess them, and not for ours only, but for any number who will avail themselves of it in the way pointed out. This ought to give confidence to any sinner in coming for salvation, and encourage any Christian in his desires and aims to be holy. In the atonement there is no lack. If there is any lack, it is in us, in not confessing our sins, and so receiving the benefit of the blood of Christ.

3-6. OBEDIENCE THE FRUIT AND EVIDENCE OF A LOVING KNOWLEDGE OF GOD.

How shall we know that we have availed ourselves of the propitiation of Christ, have really his advocacy, and are in union and fellowship with him? The writer might speak of the evidence of an inward witness (5: 10; Rom. 8: 16), but he chooses to cite here the evidence of character and disposition to distinguish those who have entered into the true effects of the atonement, and not in mere name confessed their sins. The connection (καὶ) of the present section with the foregoing thoughts is thus explained.

3. Hereby. *Herein*, or, *in this.* **We do know that we know him.** Have come to a knowledge of him; the tense (perfect) including past and present, *have known and still know.* It is difficult to decide whether 'him,' the object of the knowing, refers to God the Father or to Christ the Son. The exegetes are much divided on the point. We think the reference is to the Son. For, 1. That is the most obvious and immediate antecedent. 2. When the keeping of *his* commandments and *his* word is spoken of in the context, it is more natural to think of the commands and word of Christ, especially after the very significant usage in John 14: 15, 21, 23; 15: 10, 14. These parallel passages in the Gospel of John decide the reference with great certainty. The express mention of God, when occasion calls for it, in verse 5, confirms our view. Nor does the change of pronoun (from αὐτός to ἐκεῖνος) at the close of ver. 6 weaken our position, since Christ is there thought of in a remote condition—namely, on earth in the flesh—and some increased emphasis is to be expressed. Of course, knowledge of the Son involves knowledge of the Father likewise, but the particular reference is to the Son. The knowing that we know denotes the coming of assurance into Christian experience. The apostle had before told us how we can

4 He that saith, I know him, and keepeth not his commandments, is a liar, and the truth is not in him. | 4 his commandments. He that saith, I know him,

come into immediate fellowship and acquaintance with Father and Son. We must take the sins that rise in consciousness, and spread them before the Lord as Hezekiah did Sennacherib's letter. (Isa. 37: 14.) Instantly the blood of Jesus is applied, and, conscious of cleansing, we enter at once into divine fellowship and spiritual knowledge. This knowledge becomes assured by certain evidence. As to knowing Christ, there is a kind of knowledge that impenitent men have, a knowledge from report. But when one through confession and atoning blood is justified, he has fellowship with the Son, and knows him personally; knows *him*, and not merely something *about* him; and knows him with the affections, with a common uniting life. When we know a fact we receive it into our minds, our being; when we know Christ truly we receive him into our minds, our being. "The object of this knowing becomes the substance of him that knows." (Lange.) Intimate knowledge, because true knowledge, the knowledge of union; the knowledge of actual taste, experience. This meaning of the word (γινώσκω) is common to John. It is a pervasive idea in our Epistle. Compare John 17: 3. Green says, when knowledge involves experience, this is the word (γινώσκω, not οἶδα) always used in the New Testament. (Eph. 3: 19; Phil. 3: 10.) Now such knowledge of Christ is more or less self-evidencing. But there is confirming evidence beyond itself. We know that we have this knowledge, **if we keep his commandments.** This is the evidence implied in the word 'hereby,' which opens the sentence. 'Commandments.' Those found in the gospel of our Saviour, including, on the one hand, the spiritual duties of Christians to each other, and on the other, the precepts which Christ gave respecting his two simple ordinances. "Love one another" is a sample of the former. "Arise, and be baptized" and "Take, eat; this is my body" are specimens of the latter. Neither the outward observance nor the inner spiritual duty, imposed by Christ, is to be disregarded. Neither is unimportant. The disciple of Jesus is certainly bound to obey one as well as the other. He has no discretion in the way of selection or variation. Christ's will is paramount as to any gospel command. **Keep.** To keep the Lord's commands involves three distinct things: 1. To regard them with watchful interest and approval. 2. To guard and preserve them as something precious. 3. To do them, to obey them. The disciple is bound to exemplify the full meaning of the word, in relation to any command of Christ. (Ps. 103: 18.) Now John puts forth this keeping of the gospel commands as a proof of acquaintance with Christ. By this, in the way of deduction or inference, shall ye know that ye know him. But we think there is a further important truth implied—namely, that this keeping of the commands reacts upon the knowing act itself, and clarifies it. It is a means of becoming more definitely conscious of the divine fellowship, or of the blessing God gives. There is nothing so sure to clear away doubts from the mind as coming into practical relation to a positive command of Christ. Spiritual knowledge, at first dim and uncertain, is realized in the doing of the Lord's will, so far as we know it; according to the words in Isa. 1: 19; Ps. 119: 100; John 7: 17. It is to those who obey him that God gives clear knowledge and assurance. Some who have begun to believe, are longing and praying for more evidence of their conversion. They are in pain about it. Now let their little faith begin to act in a way of obedience to gospel commands, and they shall have their desire. Objectively by deduction, and subjectively by intuition, they shall know that they know the Lord. The light of life comes in following Christ. (John 8: 12.) By this the blessing of believers' baptism, so often testified of, may be, in part at least, understood. It is God's occasion of revealing the light of life more abundantly in the soul, according to the principle of our passage. They who will have all their light before obedience reverse the divine order, and the light professed is without its credentials. "The Gnostics, by the Spirit's prescient forewarning, are refuted, who boasted of knowledge, but set aside obedience." (Fausset.)

4. He that saith, etc. Such a person *says* what is not true. He is likewise acting a lie. He is not true to the relation in which he professes to be. Believers deny their very nature if they do not obey gospel commands. To

5 But whoso keepeth his word, in him verily is the love of God perfected: hereby know we that we are in him.
6 He that saith he abideth in him ought himself also so to walk, even as he walked.

and keepeth not his commandments, is a liar, and
5 the truth is not in him: but whoso keepeth his word,
in him verily hath the love of God been perfected.
6 Hereby know we that we are in him: he that saith
he abideth in him ought himself also to walk even
as he walked.

know the Lord, and to disregard his will, are a contradiction. **And the truth is not in him.** Not a mere repetition, in a negative form, that the person lies; but a more radical and condemnatory statement, that he is utterly lacking in the gospel principle, the new nature, the true religion. See note on 1: 8.

5. In him verily is the love of God perfected. The term 'verily' (ἀληθῶς) here means not only in reality, but also, in accordance with the principle of truth in the new man; harmonizing naturally somewhat with the similar word "truth" (ἀλήθεια) just before used. 'In him' is literally *in this one*—namely, the one who keeps Christ's word. "The love of God" is not God's love to us (Bengel), nor ours to him (Neander), nor the reciprocal love between him and us (Ebrard), nor the love commanded by God (Episcopius), but the principle of spiritual love in us which is of God as its source and as to its nature (4: 7, 8), and which is shed abroad in our hearts by the Holy Ghost given unto us. (Rom. 5: 5.) It is God's love in us; the divine element imparted to us. It is the element of the fountain found in the stream. It is not the same thing as the knowledge in ver. 3, though the spiritual knowledge of Christ and this love of God imply and mutually interpenetrate each other, and do not exist apart, in the regenerate man. This love is perfected in us as we keep the word of Christ. It is developed, matured, completed, brought to its true end and fullness, through obedience. Evangelical obedience is the carrying out and completion of love itself. The important doctrine is taught, that the keeping of positive commands is necessary to the completeness of the inner life. The tree is not complete till it bears fruit; neither is our Christian life. Query: Is not the relation of faith and baptism in Mark 16: 16 the same as that of love and obedience in this verse of John? **Hereby know we that we are in him.** 'Hereby,' *herein*—that is, in this love, enlarged and matured by obedience, this being the thought that immediately precedes. 'In him' is in Christ. See note on ver. 3. This is according to the analogy of New Testament doctrine, that believers should be in Christ, while Christ is in the Father, and so our application of the pronouns in ver. 3 is confirmed. Being in Christ is one of the deepest facts of our Christian standing. It means vital union with him, as the branch is in the vine (John 15: 5), as the members are in the body. (Eph. 5: 30.) It is not a moral or sympathetic union; but a spiritual union, a union of life. In him and us there is one life. That life depends in us upon the one Holy Spirit, by whom the union is effected and maintained. (1 Cor. 6: 17: 12: 13.) This union, as our passage teaches, may be a matter of assured knowledge on the part of those who have come into it.

6. Abideth in him. That is, in Christ. See John 15: 4, 6, and 1 John 2: 28; 3: 6 for plain references of this expression to Christ; also our interpretation of the pronoun in ver. 3, 5. Proof of the reference is cumulative. The term 'abideth' is the strongest assertion of the permanency of the state of union with Christ. **Ought himself also so to walk, even as he walked.** The pronoun referring to Christ is changed (from αὐτὸς to ἐκεῖνος), because he is for the moment viewed more remotely in his earthly life, and because it is thus that the emphatic distinction between the subjects of the verbs, between the disciple and the exemplar, can be represented. He who claims to be in union with Christ ought 'himself' (αὐτός) to walk in the path of loving obedience as that one (ἐκεῖνος) walked therein. 'That one' was in union with the Father, and did his commands. If we are in union with the Son, let us do his commands out of divine union and love (John 14: 15; 15: 10), copying the example of his own obedience in its exactness (Matt. 3: 15) and cheerfulness. (John 4: 34.)

7-11. A LEADING COMMAND TO BE KEPT BY THE CHRISTIAN, AS EVIDENCE OF HAVING COME INTO GOD'S LIGHT, IS THE ONE WHICH ENJOINS BROTHERLY LOVE.

Men have been happy, yet deceived at the same time as to their spiritual standing. There is a far more certain evidence of hav-

7 Brethren, I write no new commandment unto you,
but an old commandment which ye had from the beginning.
The old commandment is the word which ye
have heard from the beginning.
8 Again, a new commandment I write unto you,

7 Beloved, no new commandment write I unto you,
but an old commandment which ye had from the
beginning: the old commandment is the word which
8 ye heard. Again, a new commandment write I unto
you, which thing is true in him and in you; because

ing come into God's light, and that is a heart to obey the gospel commands. Following Christ, doing his word, walking as he walked—this declares the new nature, and perfects the divine love in us. The apostle having thus set the positive gospel commands in their true relation to the Christian life, it is natural for him to recall one of those commands in particular, and dwell upon its power to disclose our religious state.

7. Brethren. The great textual critics, Lachmann, Tischendorf, Tregelles, Westcott and Hort, substitute the word *beloved* for 'brethren,' in this place. This epithet naturally introduces some expressions on the love commandment. It recognizes those addressed as persons who have entered into the circle of the divine love, and are especially dear to God and his people. It marks John's own feeling toward them. Standing in this relation to him, he could be the surer of their interest in what he was about to urge, and of their faithful application of it. **I write no new commandment unto you, but an old commandment which ye had from the beginning.** After all the varying and elaborate opinions, written in the books, on the reference of the word 'commandment' (ἐντολή, *something enjoined*) in this place, we regard the passages 3: 11 and 2 John 5: 6 as proving that John means by it the injunction of his Lord, that we should love one another. That this command was pre-eminent in John's mind is shown both by his own writings and by tradition. See Godet, "Com. on the Gospel of John," vol. I., p. 61. His readers would be already familiar with it, and with his emphasis of it. To remind them of it, he needed not in every case to express it. The remotest reference would be understood. A particular command referred to, if not expressly named, would immediately call to mind the oft-repeated paramount one relating to brotherly love. Possibly there had been some discussion among the readers as to the proper description of this commandment, whether it should be called old or new. If so, the somewhat abrupt justification of either term is accounted for, and the readers would be all the more aware just what commandment was intended. This commandment, though often designated as new, was yet old. It was no recent innovation, no novelty; but was prominent in the earliest preaching that had come to the churches. From the beginning of their acquaintance with the Christian message, they had had before them the love commandment. It was therefore old; not in the sense that the earth and the skies are old; but in the sense that the message of the gospel was already long familiar. Christ himself had said, "This is my commandment, that ye love one another, as I have loved you." It was his particular injunction, and ever since his day, for scores of years, it had been echoing through the churches. **Which ye have heard.** This suggests how they had come into possession of this sweet law of Christ. It was not their discovery, but a revelation, a testimony, brought to them by the apostles. They heard it from without, when they began their life in the faith. The repetition of the words, 'from the beginning,' at the close of the verse, should be omitted.

8. Again, a new commandment I write unto you. The word 'again,' is simply the introduction of another form of statement. "I have stated," says the writer, "that the command is old; but again I have to say that it is new as well. Jesus himself so entitled it." (John 13: 34.) "And I do not wish"—so John would say—"to deny the lasting name he gave to it. On the other hand, I would retain the precious name, and all that it means." When we consider John's union of thinking with his Lord, his authorship of the gospel bearing his name, and the undoubted familiarity of his readers with his Lord's precepts, it seems impossible to suppose that the new commandment here can be other than that named in John 13: 34. Neither John nor his readers could think of anything else when that expression was employed. How common to the line of New Testament thought is the precept relating to brotherly love may be understood by consulting John 13: 34, 35; 15: 12, 17; Rom. 12: 10; 13: 8; Eph. 5: 2;

which thing is true in him, and in you: because the darkness is past, and the true light now shineth.
9 He that saith he is in the light, and hateth his brother, is in darkness even until now.

the darkness is passing away, and the true light al-
9 ready shineth. He that saith he is the light, and
hateth his brother, is in the darkness even until now.

1 Thess. 4: 9; 1 Peter 1: 22; 2: 17; 4: 8, and the many references in John's Epistles. Why is it called a 'new' commandment? Because it inculcated, as no previous commandment had done, a duty founded on the exclusive and peculiar relation of Christians to each other as spiritual kinsmen of Christ, children of the new birth, and members of God's elect family. The general duty of love from man to man, the neighborly and benevolent feeling that all men should have towards one another, had been long since enjoined. This commandment was as old as the law itself. But the peculiar love which the regenerate have for each other, through the promptings of the new life of Christ in them—such love, in fact, as Christ had for his own disciples, as distinguished from others—was first brought to light as a distinct duty, and made the subject of a command in the Gospel Dispensation, and within the gospel sphere. As Christ's feelings towards his own were different from those he felt towards others, and as members of the same earthly family feel towards each other an interest and affection which they cannot feel for others, so will Christ have the members of his spiritual family cherish the family interest and affection which their new relation of kinship calls for; and the command expressing this will is a new command. Brotherly love, in the meaning of Christ and his apostles, is the family grace. Christ first announced it, enjoined it. A fresh commandment indeed, marking the New Dispensation, and the intimate kinship of the redeemed people under it. It is something of which the world knows nothing. It is new with Christians. **Which thing.** Not the commandment, but that which is predicated of it—to wit, its character of newness; or, it may be, the fact that it was a new one. **Is true.** Is realized and fulfilled; becomes actual truth, a feature of the truth system, reflecting God's own nature of light. **In him.** In Christ; in him who gave the new commandment. The pronoun 'him,' introduced as it is, without any expressed antecedent, indicates that the writer's mind is full of the thought of Christ in connection with the new commandment. And what new commandment should so readily connect itself with Christ, in the mind of John, as the command to love one another? Hence this is the one which most naturally falls into our verse, though unexpressed. Its character of newness is true in him, since he first realized it in his peculiar love to his people; and it was true in the disciples addressed, since they were among the first to realize it among themselves. They and he had tested it, and knew it. With them the new commandment was fulfilled as a reality; they were its living examples; it was new in them. **Because the darkness is past** (or, *is passing away*) **and the true light now shineth.** It is time, therefore, for the new commandment, and to expect its illustrations in Christ, and in a people related to him. It is time for the realization of what has just been said of it. It corresponds to the period. The gospel day has been opened. Christ has come, the light of God, the shining holiness of God himself; and now all that believe in him partake of that light. The new life, by the Holy Spirit, abounds. It works, it must work, in the way of brotherly love. Where light is there is love, in God's nature, in man's. And in so far as God's light comes, moral darkness flees away. The true light is the genuine, ultimate light, of which all other is the type. Compare the true vine in John 15: 1. On 'light' and 'darkness,' see note on 1: 5. It is remarkable that in the Sanscrit, Greek, Latin. Teutonic, and Celtic tongues, God is named from the day, sky, or shining light.

9. He that saith. His *saying* does not weigh or prevail against the moral fact. Profession against truth is lighter than air. **He is in the light**—in the light of God's nature—that is, regenerate, a child of light. "In the community of light." (Ebrard.) **Hateth his brother.** The brother here is one's Christian brother, a kinsman in Christ, a fellow-partaker of the light-nature; and hence the object of the peculiar love prescribed in the new commandment. This command, as we have seen (ver. 8), is for the children of God. "It prescribes the affec-

10 He that loveth his brother abideth in the light, and there is none occasion of stumbling in him.
11 But he that hateth his brother is in darkness, and walketh in darkness, and knoweth not whither he goeth, because that darkness hath blinded his eyes.

10 He that loveth his brother abideth in the light, and
11 there is none occasion of stumbling in him. But he
that hateth his brother is in the darkness, and walketh in the darkness, and knoweth not whither he
goeth, because the darkness hath blinded his eyes.

tion which Christians are to entertain towards each other as distinguished from other men." (Hackett, MS. notes.) However benevolent and kind the world's people are, they know nothing, experimentally, of the brotherly love of the community of light. But the Christian *must* know it, and exercise it toward a brother, else he denies his professed light-nature. If he lives in a state of hatred towards a brother, he is outside of the light of God, which is also his love. He denies the very love-nature of God. He has no recognizable evidence of being a child of light, a converted man. See 3: 14. How shall we love God, and not be in union with our kind? Hatred belongs to the region of darkness, foreign to God, the realm of sin. In ver. 3 John had applied the commandment test in general. He now applies a particular command—namely, the new one, and judges a Christian by it. **Until now.** Though gospel light has been shining many years, yet through it all, up to this very moment, and notwithstanding whatsoever profession, that man is in his sins. In the Greek, the word for 'darkness' has the article prefixed, as is usual with familiar abstract nouns. See T. S. Green's "N. T. Grammar," p. 16.

10. He that loveth his brother. With the peculiar love required in the new command—a love like that of Christ to his own. The converted do have a peculiar love to Christians; a tenderness, a spirit of forgiveness and forbearance towards them, a delight in them, a feeling of union with them utterly inexpressible. **Abideth in the light.** Abides consciously in it, through the cherishing of this love. He has the evidence of being in God's light, and realizes it. It is perhaps suggested that one way of losing this evidence is to neglect or violate brotherly love. Such neglect or violation destroys one's good feelings, corrodes the new life, kills the sense of fellowship with God, damages and darkens the whole religious life, and must dissipate Christian evidence. But if brotherly love continue, the sense of God's love continues. It is a great thing to *abide* in the sense of union and communion with him. **There is none occasion of stumbling in him.** There is not a stumbling-block (σκάνδαλον), an offense, in him—that is, in the one who loves his brother. There is nothing in him to cause himself or another to fall. He may have faults, but they will be so covered (Prov. 10: 12; 1 Peter 4: 8) or neutralized, or extenuated, by the presence of superabounding love, as to do little harm, and it will make easy the overcoming of offending things. A consistent life is easy where love is. But how the harboring of the spirit of hate towards a brother affects unfavorably, not only the person who persists in it, but others around him, both saints and sinners, while it lends to his other faults a doubly offensive power!

11. Is in darkness and walketh in darkness. (John 11: 9, 10; 12: 35.) Not only is the hater of his brother in the darkness of sin and error personally, but all his movements and ways in religion are those of a man who walks in the dark. There is not the firm tread, the confidence, the decision, the ease, the clearness of view, the straightness of course, of one who walks in the light of day. The groping, blind man is his picture. How he feels his way! how uncertain his gait! how little prepared to avoid the flying arrow! How solicitous we are as he nears the edge of danger! He is at the mercy of circumstances. He cannot command himself. Such is the image of one who allows any unrepented sin, but particularly that of brotherly hatred, to lie upon his heart, plunging him into darkness. **Knoweth not whither he goeth.** (Eccl. 10: 15.) He cannot see his own path; he cannot see ahead; is uncertain where he will bring up at last; cannot tell exactly where he is. Why is this so? The last clause answers. **Because that darkness hath blinded his eyes.** *Blinded*, not 'hath blinded,' is the exact sense. Blinded them at the first sin, though the state then begun, has continued. Nothing is more blinding to the spiritual eyesight than hatred. It will take away one's power of discerning the right and truth of a case. He will be blind to whatever is redeeming in the one he hates. He cannot perceive the foolishness and inconsistency of his own

12 I write unto you, little children, because your sins are forgiven you for his name's sake.

12 I write unto you, *my* little children, because your
13 sins are forgiven you for his name's sake. I write

conduct. How poor a figure he cuts! He seems to be blind to the spirit of the gospel and the mind of Christ. He seems to be blind even as to the nature and duty of brotherly love itself. Besides, his vision of the true meaning of God's word is necessarily impaired. The whole result accords with reason and experience as well as with Scripture. Let us be afraid of this darkening sin. It is interesting to note John's habit of circling his thoughts about great pairs of principles, or moral states—pairs of opposites which are mutually exclusive, and which do not admit of any middle ground or mean, such as light and darkness, truth and falsehood, love and hatred, life and death, the spirit and the flesh, love of the Father and love of the world. Between these principles or states in a given pair, there is no compromise, no intermingling. (2: 21.) They are strict alternatives. Alliance with one is the denial of a part in the other.

12–14. FACTS IN THE SPIRITUAL CHARACTER OF HIS READERS, WHICH ENCOURAGE THE APOSTLE TO WRITE TO THEM AS HE DOES.

John has developed a system of experimental doctrine, reaching a life reflecting the light of God's nature. Confessed sin washed away in Christ's blood; then conscious fellowship with God; then obedience, running especially in the line of the love-command. A wonderful exposition of the law of the new life! There is presented the new life in its principle, method, and outworking—its principle, union with God; its method, forgiveness of sins through Christ; its outworking, obedience and love, especially brotherly love. And now, having completed this portrait of the new kingdom, and applied it in a way to test severely the spiritual standing of his readers, the writer deems it meet to offer some words of confidence (as Heb. 6: 9) and commendation, causing them to feel that it is from no distrust of their attainments that he writes as he does, and thus saving them unnecessary despondency.

12. I write unto you. In relation to the love-duty as testing their spiritual standing—the great matter occupying his heart and pen when he begins this verse. **Little children** (τεκνία). A name of endearment, applied here by the writer to the whole circle of his Christian readers, and recalling their new birth and their childlike attributes. See note on 2: 1, and this obvious application of the word in 2: 28; 3: 18; 4: 4; 5: 21. **Because your sins are forgiven you.** True of all the Christians whom the apostle addressed. They had been forgiven, and still were a forgiven people. The assurance of this made them seem very near to the old apostle, and made writing to them a great pleasure. He had confidence in them, and therefore, with the less misgiving, could lay all the demands of the gospel, all the tests of the new life, upon them. His confidence set his pen free. The Christian pastor knows what it is to preach the great testing doctrines freely under such circumstances. And this strengthens and fortifies the good Christian against an evil day. How much more heartily, and no doubt usefully, we can preach these things, when we have confidence in the Christian character of our people, and can say so, as John did! We learn, too, that even a people walking with God needs thorough gospel teaching. What a great fact to declare concerning any of the race of sinners: 'Your sins are forgiven you'! There is such a thing as full forgiveness of sin, and John's great, endeared flock knew what it is. **For his name's sake**—literally, and with clearer meaning, *through his name*. [Rather, "on account of his name," and the name represents the person. Christ, before described as "a propitiation of sins," is here affirmed to be the ground. reason, or motive of forgiveness. And this is evidently the meaning which the author has in mind, but has not clearly expressed by the word "through." The expression is of great doctrinal significance.—A. H.] This language carries back the mind to the method of forgiveness announced in 1: 7 and 2: 1, 2. The obvious reference is to the name of Jesus Christ, who bore in himself the punishment of sin, and for whose sake God can look propitiously on each penitent soul; the name symbolizes the atoning work wrought under that name. John says '*his* name's sake,' without giving the name, because the name by which they were saved

13 I write unto you, fathers, because ye have known him *that is* from the beginning. I write unto you, young men, because ye have overcome the wicked one. I write unto you, little children, because ye have known the Father.

unto you, fathers, because ye know him who is from the beginning. I write unto you, young men, because ye have overcome the evil one. [1] I have written unto you, little children, because ye know the

1 Or, *I wrote*.

was already so deep in their knowledge and love.

13. Fathers. Having designated his readers generally by the name of 'little children,' and predicated of them the blessed fact of the forgiveness of their sins through Christ, the writer now gives more particular emphasis to his confidence by addressing them in classes according to their age, and affirms great things of either class. At the same time he wishes to forestall any possible idea of depreciation connecting itself with the name of 'little children.' You are, he would say, indeed 'little children' in your new life, humility, and relation to my heart; but in respect of strength and maturity you are men—**fathers** ripe in knowledge, **young men** strong in grace. **Ye have known him that is from the beginning.** Namely, Christ, who, though he had come in the flesh, lived in his divine nature in the beginning with God himself. (1:1; John 1:1.) Him who from everlasting was in union with the Father, they had come to know, and were by him raised to divine fellowship, and made partakers of the eternal life in him. To know Christ in the Johannean sense is something very deep and far-reaching. See note on 2:3. In this knowing, we are vitally identified or united with that which is known; we are conscious of the new life, the divine union and fellowship. There is something powerfully uplifting in this experience. In it there is a knowing of Christ, not only in his death, but as a Divine Saviour with eternal life in himself. This knowledge the 'fathers' had. **Young men.** Christians in their early manhood, a prominent class in the churches within the eye of John. He testifies that they had a vigor of Christian experience, an athletic activity, at the farthest remove from childlike weakness. They had his highest confidence. **Because.** For the causal significance, see note on ver. 12. **Have overcome the wicked one.** The word 'overcome' (νικάω) is Johannean; being used sixteen times in Revelation, six times in our Epistle, and only four times in the rest of the New Testament. The victory affirmed here corresponds well with the peculiar temptations of those in early manhood. Nearly all understand the wicked one (τὸν πονηρόν) to mean the devil, or Satan, the tempter, whose badness is so pervading that he is altogether bad. (3:12; 5:18; Matt. 13:19; Eph. 6:16.) There is victory over this strong one and the sin which he fosters. The young men had achieved it. They had done so by coming to a knowledge that their sins are forgiven, and to a consciousness of union with God. The victory implies this knowledge and union. Up to the point of such knowledge and union, Satan makes a terrible fight to possess the soul. He holds it in darkness and bondage while he can, and has power over it till it comes into the knowledge and liberty of Christ. But when that great point is reached Satan is conquered. He is not slain. He does not cease to tempt. His buffetings are often severely felt. But he is no longer owner or master. And how shall one continue his victory over Satan but by living always in the conscious acceptance of Christ? While the justifying blood renders the soul happy Satan is overcome. The young men, then, were prevalent on the basis of a gospel experience. That is the source of strength to the spiritual athlete. **I write** (*wrote*, or *have written*, ἔγραψα, aor., not γράφω, pres.,) **unto you.** All modern critics of the sacred text give us this tense of the verb. We suppose the present tense got into use from an idea that the second-named 'little children' (παιδία not τεκνία) were literally in their age child-Christians, to be co-ordinated with the two preceding classes of 'fathers' and 'young men.' This idea naturally conformed the tense of the verb, introducing a supposed third class to that of the verbs introducing the other two classes in the category; and the same idea held the whole sentence to ver. 13, instead of allowing it to introduce, as it should, ver. 14. But the manuscript authority demands the aorist form; and that indicates that the little children here addressed do not form a third class with the two preceding classes in a division of age.

14 I have written unto you, fathers, because ye have known him *that is* from the beginning. I have written unto you, young men, because ye are strong, and the word of God abideth in you, and ye have overcome the wicked one.

14 Father. [1] I have written unto you, fathers, because ye know him who is from the beginning [1] I have written unto you, young men, because ye are strong, and the word of God abideth in you, and ye have
15 overcome the evil one. Love not the world, neither

[1] Or, *I wrote.*

The change in tense introduces a new series of statements, a going over the whole matter in a changed relation of time or point of view. Why the past tense? Beza, Düsterdieck and Hackett say it is the epistolary aorist, the writing being for the moment thought of as already in the reader's hands. Others think it refers to the former part of the Epistle. The first view seems forced, and the passages cited are doubtful parallels. The second view misses the fact that the thrice-repeated 'write' relates to matter just written, and indeed to the very essence of the doctrine enunciated up to this point. We think the verb in the past tense relates to the very same matter that it did in the present tense. But that matter is viewed as a little more remote from the writer, a little farther back in the past, owing to the time elapsed since he began writing at ver. 12, or, more likely, owing to an interruption in the writing. **Little children.** The disciples in general are thus addressed by John. Here the Greek word (παιδία) is different from that rendered 'little children' before, but it means essentially the same as the other. See Matt. 18: 3, 5; John 21: 5; and note on ver. 18. It is simply a lively verbal variation. Alford and Lange maintain our view in the interest of harmony of structure and parallel correspondence in the two series of sentence. **Have known the Father.** What had been said of the spiritual knowledge of the fathers, in the former part of the verse, is true of all the disciples; knowledge of the Father and Son being essentially one.

14. He repeats his confidence in his readers, not only as a whole, but in classes. The repetition is made, because it was very pleasant to John, and it is for the sake of deepening the assurance and enlarging the testimony at some points. This testimony to the decided spiritual character of his readers is still rendered, because his testing words in relation to love and light, hatred and darkness, might seem to cast doubt upon their state. He writes, or wrote, not because he doubted them, but for the very reason that he believed well of them. Their true spiritual character encouraged him to write most searchingly and most radically. And there was the greater pleasure in writing to such as they, because they would appreciate his divine doctrine. **Because ye are strong.** As John is setting forth spiritual and not natural endowments, there can be no doubt that he testifies here to the spiritual strength of the young men, which was so appropriate at the same time to the more active period of their lives. This strength came from their sense of joyous union with the Lord. (Neh. 8: 10; Eph. 6: 10.) This is the way of strength to young and old. Strength is the unfailing product of a joyous experience of God's love—strength to do, to bear, to hold up the Saviour's name, to cope with Satan and all adversaries. **The word of God abideth in you.** Their birth into the light of God's nature synchronized with the entrance of God's word into their hearts. (Ps. 119: 130.) This word is that of the gospel, the truth of salvation by confession, and the blood of Jesus. This word became living in their regeneration. The word thus planted abides. It is no temporary principle. In it there is the principle of obedience on the one hand, and steadfastness against error on the other. All this was exemplified in those young men. And so they were victors in the contest with the wicked one.

15-17. THOSE WHO ARE FORGIVEN AND UNITED TO GOD MUST NOT LOVE THE WORLD.

Having written faithfully (3-11) to such a people as his readers were, the apostle can now warn them, and all the better, because of the confidence which he has in them and which he has just now expressed. He warns them against the worldliness which will tempt them, though so utterly foreign to their new life. They are indeed washed from their sins, are in conscious divine fellowship, are victorious over the wicked one, have the word of God abiding in them, but they are not yet taken out of the world, are still surrounded with evil, and the remains of a lustful, covetous, proud nature, are still within them. Forgiven are they, but not yet away from the scene or danger of sin. They are in the world

15 Love not the world, neither the things *that are* in the world. If any man love the world, the love of the Father is not in him.

the things that are in the world. If any man love the world, the love of the Father is not in him.

and in the flesh. Hence the need of earnest caution. Having such great and glorious things said of them as John had been saying, they might be tempted to forget their intimate connections with a worldly existence and a fleshly nature. They might imagine that with their divine attainments they could not fall into evil; that they were above temptation and worldly influence. Not so; "let him that thinketh he standeth take heed lest he fall." (1 Cor. 10: 12.) The freeing of the soul from guilt, and its elevation into the plane of God's light, do not annihilate the sinful nature. A happy spiritual attainment must not foster spiritual pride or vain confidence. There is still a law of the flesh warring against the law of the renewed mind. The new life is a plant in the midst of tares. The recognition of this fact will keep the most rejoicing Christian humble and cautious.

15. Love not the world. "Do not continue to cherish that affection so natural to men. A negative command in the present (μὴ ἀγαπᾶτε) forbids an act already begun; in the subjunctive aorist, warns against one not yet begun." (Hackett.) 'The world' here means not only the sinful ways of the world, but all objects and concerns considered as divorced from God, and as an end in themselves. It includes all that may receive attention, and become an idol to our hearts, in place of God. In the unforgiven man, worldliness is the governing principle. He loves the objects of nature, or the walks of science, or the acquisition of wealth, or the displays of fashion, or honor from men, or pleasures of society or business or family, or his own thoughts and self, better than he loves God or his will. He is absorbed in the things of this life. The world is his thought, life, and love; his great idol, to which he has surrendered himself, and now gives his strength. But having received the new life, he must cease to give this supreme place to the world, and take God into his mind and heart. He is known by the object he makes supreme, by that which his life as a totality serves. It is implied that men, from their very nature, must love something supremely. Which shall it be, God or the world? We cannot serve two masters. We cannot give our affection to the world as an end in itself, and at the same time love God as God. "But," says one, "am I not to love the world at all?" No; not as something outside of God. (Col. 3: 2; Rom. 12: 2.) You may love the beauties of nature, your own family, food and raiment, etc., in subordination to your love of God, and for his sake. It is your duty to do it; and thus doing, this world will help you to love God the more. There is a loving of the world in benevolence, to do it good, that is even God-like. (John 3: 16.) **Neither the things that are in the world.** One might claim to have given up the world as a whole, and yet cling too fondly to some one object of gratification, like Ephraim. (Hosea 7: 8 seq.) John foresees this danger, and so changes his expression from the general to the particular. One may have this idol; another, that. Let each avoid his particular idols, his peculiar indulgences. **If any man love the world.** As a sphere by itself, and for itself. **The love of the Father is not in him.** The love which has the Father for its object. The relation of the words in the conditional part of the sentence, and the alternative reasoning, call for this explanation. Here John's method of holding up two mutually excluding principles or spheres is strongly illustrated. See under ver. 11. If one love the world supremely, if worldliness is his life, his governing principle, he is not a Christian; that is all. He worships and serves the creature rather than the Creator. He cannot hold a filial relation to his Father in heaven, and treat him as a Father when immersed in any earthly idolatry. God will not give his glory to another; will not divide it with any mundane good or gratification. For God's claim, especially as a *Father*, see Mal. 1: 6. For the same alternative principle, on which John reasons, see Matt. 6: 24; Rom. 8: 5, 7; 2 Cor. 6: 15; Gal. 1: 10; James 4: 4. In this connection it is interesting to compare Paul's contrast of the two covenants, and his statement of the mutual exclusiveness of the systems of works and of grace. If one, then not the other. See Godet, "Com. on Luke" 5: 36–38, for an exposition of Christ's

16 For all that *is* in the world, the lust of the flesh,
and the lust of the eyes, and the pride of life, is not of
the Father, but is of the world.
17 And the world passeth away, and the lust there-

16 For all that is in the world, the lust of the flesh, and
the lust of the eyes, and the vainglory of life, is
17 not of the Father, but is of the world. And
the world passeth away, and the lust thereof:

thought of the exclusiveness of the old life and of the new.

16. The design of this verse is to illustrate and confirm (ὅτι) the strong assertion just before made concerning the utter incompatibility of the love of the world with the love of God. They belong to opposite spheres; they come from wholly different fountains. One is from beneath; the other from above. One is spiritual; the other fleshly. In order that Christians may better see what the love of the world is, the apostle gives specimens, or instances, of the various forms it takes. Some have thought that he intended to supply an exhaustive analysis, or description, of it. But it is only, as we think, leading exhibitions of it that he puts before us, sufficient to show its essentially grovelling and selfish nature. The writer has spoken of the objects of selfish love in the world. These objects are now singularly identified with the love itself, in the forms of lust and pride, and as such they are foreign to God. They take the character of one's selfish desire, and become of a piece with it. Or a worldly love, in the forms of lust and pride, having its end and scope wholly in the world, is put among its own objects as a part of the world, and hence foreign to God. The latter account of the case is more simple than the former. Either account explains the easy gliding of the writer's mind from the objects of love in the world to the desires which they awaken. The object and subject are a virtual unity. **The lust of the flesh.** The lust prompted by the flesh. (Gal. 5: 17.) The word 'lust' (ἐπιθυμία) here, and in the next phrase, means *longing desire*, considered as inordinate. The various appetites of the bodily nature are intended. The love of the world in some is shown by seeking as their chief good the gratification of their appetites. (Phil. 3: 19.) And here comes to view the drunkard, the glutton, the epicurean, the libertine, in their various stages. **The lust of the eyes.** What is the relation of the eyes to the desire? It is subjective. The eyes are the exciting cause or occasion of the desire. This desire is less animal and more intellectual than the former, yet no less sinful when gratified for its own sake. This form of worldly love finds supreme pleasure in those things which gratify the outward sight, such as raiment, fashion, fine horses and chariots, palaces and furniture. Nor are those things which gratify the inward sight excluded. If one lives merely to gratify his intellect in systems, problems, philosophies; if he seeks art or science for their own sake only, and not with the higher end of loving and serving God, then is he as really, as supremely a lover of the world, as the devotee of dress. **The pride of life.** 'Life' (βίος) is not the vital principle (ζωή), but rather the manner, course, and circumstance of living; one's worldly state, or attainment. It becomes the exciting cause or occasion (subjective genitive) of pride. This pride is the boastfulness, swagger, vanity, ostentation, self-gratulation so prominent with some people. It finds ample means and occasions. How it grows upon one when indulged! How plain that he loves the praise of men more than the praise of God! This world is to him the means and theatre of vanity. His mind is filled with himself, and not with his God. Unlike Paul (Gal. 6: 14), he glories in the show of this life. All this "threefold concupiscence" (Augustine), now considered, is strikingly brought to view and illustrated in the tempation of Eve (Gen. 3: 6), and in the temptation of our Lord. (Luke 4: 3-11.) **Is not of (ἐκ) the Father, but is of (ἐκ) the world.** Has its origin in the carnal nature, in the plane of this world, not in the Father; for the mind that springs from him is directed to him. He in whom worldly love prevails is not one of the children (τέκνα) of the Father. His circle of life differs as much from the life of a child of God, as the whirl of a top differs from the orbit of the sun. A man is to be judged by his prevailing desires. "John grasps down to the very foundations of moral life, when he reminds his readers of the essentially distinct origin of the love of the world and the love of God. The inmost kernel of the matter is laid bare." (Düsterdieck.)

17. And the world passeth away. Another reason why we should not love the

of: but he that doeth the will of God abideth for-ever.
18 Little children, it is the last time: and as ye have

but he that doeth the will of God abideth for-ever.
18 Little children, it is the last hour: and as ye heard

world: Worldliness is not only totally outside of God (ver. 16), but it is, as to both its objects and its desire, transient and perishing. (1 Cor. 7: 31; James 4: 14; 1 Peter 1: 24.) The passing away is not annihilation, but rather a passing along or by. It describes the act of passing off the stage, or the breaking up of a scene, in a play. In our passage, it describes the breaking up of the present order and state of things. Selfish desires and their objects will soon cease to hold their present relations, passing on and over into darkness, disappointment, and ruin. The Cosmos, the worldly order, will be broken, and for the godless soul nothing will take its place! Nothing but a disordered, dark, fragmentary state, utterly hopeless! **But he that doeth the will of God.** This is the one who loves God. (Ver. 3, 5; 5: 3; John 14: 15.) The love of God appears in its completest form when it is seen doing his will. Herein is the rounding out, the demonstration of our divine love. **Abideth forever.** Observe the present tense. He has already entered into that divine order which will not be broken up, but will increase more and more. He is united to him who passes not away. He is delivered from a perishable system. He carries with him through death and every possible shock the unchanging object of his love. The Christian will have his present God, but the sinner will not have his present world.

18-23. Attention is called to the Existing Antichrists.

The apostle has warned the members of the churches against the sin of worldliness. It was an evil of the heart to which every one of them was liable. Hence the need of the best saint walking cautiously, humbly. Having warned the obedient against the evil lurking in their own hearts, it is natural for the writer to pass next to a form of hostile influence that they must encounter in other men, even in those who claim the name of Christians, but who in reality deny Christ, and in heart are opposed to him. God's true children must be on their guard, not only against a love of the world in themselves, but against the wolves in sheep's clothing, who, professing to be Christians, teach doctrines which in effect destroy Christ. These are the hardest, most subtle, foes Christianity has to battle with, those who pretend to receive it, and at the same time are undermining it with their errors. Open infidels, opponents laying no claim to the Christian name, are not half so dangerous. The Christian religion has had more to suffer from those professing the gospel and at the same time perverting it, than from all the world besides.

18. Little children. This term (παιδία), the same as in ver. 13, applies figuratively to all the true saints, with reference especially to their dependence, their need of care and warning, and their pupil state. The other term for 'little children' (τεκνία, ver. 12), as applied to Christians, seems to suggest more their new birth and spiritual character, though the two terms practically cover very largely each other's ground. **It is the last time.** The word 'time'—literally, *hour*—designates a season having defined limits. What is meant by the last such season here announced? It must be remembered that the assertion was made eighteen hundred years ago, and was as true then as it would be if spoken to-day. Is it not said of the entire period of the Christian Church? When Christ was ascended, he gave the Holy Spirit. From that beginning was the Dispensation of the Spirit, to be continued till the last of the elect should be brought in. When the Spirit came, Peter said this was what Joel said should come to pass in the last days. In prophetical passages of the Old Testament the expression "last days" is used almost exclusively of the Messianic times. (Gen. 49: 1; Isa. 2: 2; Micah 4: 1.) The expressions "latter times" in 1 Tim. 4: 1, "last days" in 2 Tim. 3: 1, Heb. 1: 2, "last times" in 1 Peter 1: 20, "last time" in Jude 18, "ends of the world" in 1 Cor. 10: 11, "end of the world" in Heb. 9: 26, appear from their context to designate the whole gospel period. It is the last stage of the world's religious history. There is to be no other season of salvation, no added forces of redemption in some after era. The theory of some that another more powerful Dispensation is yet to come for the men of the world is virtually denied. Now is the 'last time,'

heard that antichrist shall come, even now are there
many antichrists; whereby we know that it is the last
time.
19 They went out from us, but they were not of us;

that antichrist cometh, even now have there arisen
many antichrists; whereby we know that it is the
19 last hour. They went out from us, but they were

the last hour. This is the last Dispensation. The great ingatherings of Gentiles or Jews are to take place in it, and not beyond it. **And as ye have heard that antichrist shall come.** They *heard* (aorist) it at the outset under apostolic teaching. *Comes*—not 'shall come'—is the present of ordained fixity, prophetic fixity. (Alford.) Is not the continuous appearance, or continually recurring appearance, of antichrist, or antichrists, characterizing the Christian period, suggested in this present tense? 'Antichrist' is a name used only in John's Epistles (ver. 22; 4: 3; 2 John 7), though the doctrine of antichrist is in other passages, such as 2 Thess. 2: 3-7; 1 Tim. 4: 1-3; 2 Peter 2: 1-3. The term, in its Greek composition, may mean exclusively an adversary of Christ, or it may mean one instead of Christ and by consequence against him. The prefix (ἀντί) signifies *over against;* and one can be over against the truth under the Christian name, or repudiating it; against it in name and act, or claiming to represent it and to stand for it, yet denying it. The connection in which John treats the subject shows clearly that his idea of antichrist is that of one who in some sense stands instead of Christ; taking the Christian name yet opposing that very kingdom of truth which the name implies. We think that Paul's and Peter's doctrine implies the same conception of antichrist. This antichrist may be, when fully developed (2 Thess. 2: 3), a collective body of spiritual opposition falsely claiming the Christian name, or the leader of such a body. But the apostles had taught that though this man of sin, claiming true religion, but yet destroying it, should be fully developed near the second coming of Christ, yet he would have his forerunners, his types, all the way through the Gospel Dispensation. After referring to this antichrist Paul declares, "The mystery of iniquity doth already work"; which quite accords with John's teaching, "Ye heard that antichrist comes; even now many antichrists have arisen." And this fact that antichrists had already appeared was proof that the last decisive Dispensation had come: **Whereby we know that it is the last time.** The era of these characters is the world's last era. The rise of such men in the gospel epoch is a part of prophecy and fact, and the churches must not be disappointed or shocked by it. Here, then, is our idea of what an antichrist is. It is a false teacher of the gospel; one who while professing to believe the gospel, so perverts it as to destroy it. It is the subtle teacher of falsehood in Christianity's name. The fiercest opposition is within the temple of God, and in the name of God. (2 Thess. 2: 4.) It is not the professed atheist, or infidel, who is an antichrist. Those mentioned by John were professors of Christ, and still held to him in their way. Their portrait is in Acts 20: 30, and in the dark colors of Jude. Labeling themselves with the Christian name; saying and doing, it may be, many Christian things,—they are the most dangerous foes of the truth. They catch the unwary and inexperienced, while they teach errors that go to subvert Christianity, and to ruin the souls of men. From the days of the apostles till now, the Gospel and the Church have had this covert opposition, and even now there are many antichrists. The apostles have forewarned us of it all. It is a part of the cost to count in entering into Christian relations. It is something inevitably incident to an advancing gospel. Let us not be dismayed. The struggle is not doubtful.

19. They went out from us. Said of the antichrists, the false teachers of Christian doctrine. So far as the philology is concerned, the going out (ἐξῆλθον) may mean the going forth of these persons upon their mission as professed Christian teachers (see 4: 1), or may mean their going out from the fellowship of the true Christian body, separating themselves. The latter meaning is the true one, as the whole tenor of the verse makes evident. Whether they went out because pressed out, or wholly of their own motion, does not appear. Though disagreeing with the main body of Christians, and separated, they still claimed to interpret the Christian doctrine, and evidently professed to be Christian teachers, and, indeed, the true ones, else they

for if they had been of us, they would *no doubt* have
continued with us: but *they went out*, that they might
be made manifest that they were not all of us.
20 But ye have an unction from the Holy One, and
ye know all things.

not of us; for if they had been of us, they would
have continued with us: but *they went out*, that they
might be made manifest [1]how that they all are not
20 of us. And ye have an anointing from the Holy
21 One, [2]and ye know all things. I have not written

1 Or, *that not all are of us*......2 Some very ancient authorities read *and ye all know*.

could have had no power of seduction over Christian minds (ver. 26); and the injunction to try the spirits (4: 1-3) would have been altogether needless. Persons who stood forth as direct opponents of Christianity, outside of the Christian pale, were already distinguished, and needed no testing; and such would scarcely come under the head of deceivers—for they played no false part, wore no mask. **But they were not of us.** And they never were. (Matt. 7: 23; John 6: 70; Acts 8: 21.) 'From us,' in the preceding sentence, and 'of us,' here, are the same (*ἐξ ἡμῶν*) in the Greek. But the former, with its verb of motion, has a local meaning; while the latter, with its verb of being, has a meaning of spiritual derivation, affinity, or relationship. These men had no vital sympathy with the Church of Christ. They had taken the Christian name, but had never had the Christian nature. **For if they had been of us,** etc. The words **no doubt,** do not belong in the sentence, and the statement is stronger without them. The statement is explicit, that if those men had been true Christians, they would have abode in Christian union and fellowship, they would have remained **with us** (*μεθ' ἡμῶν*) in doctrine and association. Their defection was proof that they did not belong with the true flock (Matt. 7: 15), and the doctrine is implied that truly regenerate men do not depart from the essential Christian faith, or the associate life of the Christian Church. They do not will to depart. They are kept. **But** [they did not remain with us] **that.** The telic 'that'—*in order that* (ἵνα), dependent on an obvious idea shaped by the last verb, expresses the purpose, not of the seceders, but of God who suffered their action to take place, and who makes the wrath of man to praise him. "A design which should be accomplished according to God's counsel." (Ebrard.) **They might be made manifest that they were not all of us.** [Better, *that they all were not of us.* The negative particle modifies the verb, instead of the word "all," and the sense is, that none of them were of us.—A. H.] This is the divine purpose. The language is difficult to handle. The apostle begins with the actual seceders as the subject of the verb 'manifested,' and goes on to declare in what light they are manifested, as not being of the true flock; but before he completes the declaration, he compounds with it the further idea that those generally who claim to be of this flock are not all of it; and the course of the seceders manifests the fact by tending to distinguish those who are genuine, and those who are not. "The construction is a mixed one, compounded of two—(1) that they may be manifested that not are they of us; (2) that it may be manifested that not are all of us," though they may profess to be. (Alford.) So Lücke, Düsterdieck, Huther, Lange, Ebrard. Compare the teachings of 1 Cor. 11: 19. There is then (1) the general fact, well for us to know, that there are the spurious among the true in the Church, (2) the fact that the spurious will prove and declare themselves sooner or later, (3) the fair implication that so proving themselves, their separation is to be desired. As false doctrines (ver. 22) was that which most of all separated these men, we find it does make a difference what a man believes; that though one profess to be a Christian, yet his doctrines may be such as to show that he cannot be a Christian. He may be amiable, gifted, apparently devoted, yet there are errors of doctrine which, if he believes them, show that he is not a child of God. In other words, the Christian standing of a man is to be tested by his doctrines, as well as his life. It does make a difference, or signify a difference, even with a man's heart, what he believes.

20. But (while all this is true of the false ones) **ye** (emphatic, in opposition to the false ones, the antichrists) **have an unction from the Holy One.** They pretend to be of the anointed (*χριστοί*), while ye have the anointing (*χρῖσμα*) indeed. 'Unction' is not the act of anointing, but the anointing oil, an emblem and name of the Holy Spirit, by whose bestowal

21 I have not written unto you because ye know not the truth, but because ye know it, and that no lie is of the truth.
22 Who is a liar but he that denieth that Jesus is the Christ? He is antichrist, that denieth the Father and the Son.

unto you because ye know not the truth, but because ye know it, and [1] because no lie is of the truth.
22 Who is the liar but he that denieth that Jesus is
the Christ? This is the antichrist, *even* he that de-
23 nieth the Father and the Son. Whosoever denieth

1 Or, *that*.

on believers they are made kings, prophets, and priests unto God, and are one in life with Father and Son. 'The Holy One,' from whom believers have this gift, is, in this place, Christ. (Luke 1: 35; Acts 3: 14.) Christ has the Holy Spirit without measure (John 3: 34), is anointed with the oil of gladness above his fellows. (Heb. 1: 9), and this he gives to his true people. From him his members receive the unction. (Ps. 133: 2.) And there is a sense in which they receive it from the Father, inasmuch as Christ himself does. **And ye know all things.** The Holy Spirit which ye have enables you to do so. (John 14: 26; 16: 13.) [It may be fairly doubted whether the promise of Christ in John 16: 13 was meant for all Christians in the same sense, or to the same extent, as far as knowledge is concerned, as for the apostles. It included inspiration for the latter. See "Commentary on John."—A. H.] The knowing (οἴδατε) is the result of seeing with the spiritual eye opened by the Holy Spirit. The knowledge is qualitative, not quantitative; the knowing of nature, not extension. The knowledge is the same in kind with that which we have of Father and Son. (Luke 10: 22.) "The quality of an infinity we may know, even when we cannot know its quantity." (Joseph Cook.) The knowledge is the spiritual discerning of 1 Cor. 2: 14. It is the discriminative knowledge of John 7: 17. It recognizes the truth when it sees it, and distinguishes it from falsehood and error. It has an eye for it; knows it as the bee knows the honey. Of course, John is thinking mainly of the doctrines of religion as the object of this knowledge; and he teaches that a God-taught (1 Thess. 4: 9) mind cannot depart far into error. It will know the vital truths; and, knowing them, will adhere to them. If this is true of all the converted, it makes them one in the essential faith.

21. John again (see on ver. 12) assures his readers that it is not from distrust of them, but from hearty confidence, that he wrote (ἔγραψα) the plain things now before them; having *now* in mind particularly his admonition concerning the antichrists. It is because they know the truth (reflection or image of God's nature), and its utter antagonism to falsehood, that he can have courage and hope to write to them. He feels that they will understand and appreciate his words, and rightly use them for their good, contrasting, in this respect, with the unspiritual, unknowing errorists. **By truth** and **life** he describes the doctrinal positions of the anointed and the antichrists respectively, and their utter mutual exclusiveness in origin and matter.

22. The apostle proceeds to tell us what the 'lie,' the chief error, of the false teachers is. **Who is a** (literally, *the*) **liar?** The article *the* marks its substantive as one that has been already expressly or impliedly mentioned. "Implication in the word *lie*, ver. 21." (T. S. Green, "Gram. N. T.," p. 13.) Paraphrase: "I have spoken of a lie, I have said virtually that somebody has been lying; now, who is the liar?" Instead of asking, "What is the lie?" the writer passes vividly from the general abstract to the definite concrete and asks, "Who (implying *what*) is the liar?" We might also say that the implication of the word is in the term *antichrists* as far back as ver. 18. **But** (or, *except*, εἰ μὴ) depends on an implied negative answer to the question—**He that denieth that Jesus is the Christ.** The negative (οὐκ) in the original text is explained by supposing the proposition to be the tenor, or form, of the denial. The denying is to this effect, or in these terms, that Jesus is not the Christ. For idiom, see Luke 20: 27; Gal. 5: 17; Heb. 12: 19. This position was held in two forms (1), that Jesus Christ was not literal man (4: 2), and the humanity being denied, the Messiahship was denied, since the former was necessary to the latter; (2) that Jesus and the Logos were only temporarily and, as it were, mechanically connected; and as the Logos and the Messiah were held to be essentially identical, so Jesus could not be the Christ, or Messiah. See history of the Gnostic Cerinthus. Jesus might be accepted in a sense; and so Christ, in a sense;

23 Whosoever denieth the Son, the same hath not the Father: [*but*] *he that acknowledgeth the Son hath the Father also.*
24 Let that therefore abide in you, which ye have heard from the beginning. If that which ye have heard from the beginning shall remain in you, ye also shall continue in the Son, and in the Father.

the Son, the same hath not the Father: he that con-
24 fesseth the Son hath the Father also. As for you,
let that abide in you which ye heard from the beginning. If that which ye heard from the beginning abide in you, ye also shall abide in the Son,
25 and in the Father. And this is the promise which

but that Jesus was the Christ was denied. **He is antichrist.** Better, *This is the antichrist.* (Revised Version.) This one who denies that Jesus is the Christ is to be identified with the (already mentioned) antichrist. **That denieth the Father and the Son.** Appositional clause further defining the antichrist, equivalent to even he that denieth, etc. (Revised Version.) To deny that Jesus is the Christ is to deny the Son of God, since the Son is Jesus Christ. And to deny the Sonship is to deny God's natural relation to Christ as Father. Hence, Father and Son are both denied. God's great reason for having the name of Father is his relation to his Son. If that relation be denied, the Fatherhood in its deepest sense is denied. Besides, God the Father is manifested, and is understood, only through the Son. (Matt. 11: 27.) Strange that the deniers of Christ's true nature do not see that their error invades and mars the true nature of God himself. It is a generic, far-reaching lie, affecting the whole system of truth; and the words of John Newton will come for utterance:

> What think ye of Christ? is the test
> To try both your state and your scheme;
> You cannot be right in the rest,
> Unless you think rightly of him.

23. The same hath not the Father. Every one who denies the Son is evidently destitute of him, and of the Father also. To be without the Son is to be without the Father, for the Father is in the Son. (John 14: 9.) Not to have the Father means not to have union or communion with him or inheritance in him. *(But)* **he that acknowledgeth** (*confesseth*, as in the Revised Version, is the better rendering) **the Son, hath the Father also.** The translators of our Common Version doubted the genuineness of these words, hence their italics. Later criticism puts them into the true text. The *confessing* is the opposite of the denial; and it is open, express confession, such as Rom. 10: 9; Matt. 10: 32; Luke 12: 8 and John 12: 32 emphasize the necessity of. Nor is it such a confession in a mere intellectual way, but in a spiritual way, and from the centre of the soul. That confession secures the Son, and with him all the riches of the Father.

24-29. ABIDING IN THE TRUTH AND ABIDING IN THE BLESSINGS OF THE NEW LIFE GO TOGETHER.

Having spoken of the position of the deceiving antichrists, and of the doctrinal disaster and utter spiritual impoverishment involved in it, John turns to his readers, sound in faith, and exhorts them in the spirit of loving confidence.

24. Let that therefore abide in you, etc. The Revised Version is more exact: *As for you, let that abide in you which ye heard from the beginning.* The original sentence is not completed, as the opening words might lead one to expect. But it is so constructed as to make the pronoun emphatic: Ye, on your part, in contrast with the false teachers. **From the beginning** is explained at ver. 7. What they heard from that time is the apostolic doctrine, especially that denied by the antichrists. 'In you' is in the place of emphasis. What they heard with the outward ear, the apostle exhorts them to have, without change, in living union with their hearts. "Keep it," he says, "rooted fast in warm convictions, against all perversions of the antichrists." How often John recalls, and uses for himself, words from his well-remembered Saviour's lips! This word *abide*, with its deep adjunct 'in you' (compare John 15: 1-10), is an example. **If that which ye have heard from the beginning shall remain in you, ye also shall continue in the Son, and in the Father.** The words 'remain' and 'continue' represent the same original verb as the word 'abide' in the first clause; and the Revised Version does well in giving it the same rendering in every instance. 'Ye also,' as well as the true doctrine. If the true doctrine of the Son and Father (note the order of persons, order of faith and experience) abides in you, ye in turn shall abide in them; the truth in you, you in the Son and

25 And this is the promise that he hath promised us, *even* eternal life.
26 These things have I written unto you concerning them that seduce you.
27 But the anointing which ye have received of him abideth in you, and ye need not that any man

26 he promised [1] us, *even* the life eternal. These things
have I written unto you concerning them that
27 would lead you astray. And as for you, the anointing which ye received of him abideth in you, and

[1] Some ancient authorities read *you*.

Father; the truth in living union with you, you in living union with them. The truth abiding in us, and we abiding in the highest spiritual blessings; these go together. Divine union and fellowship are connected with a right doctrinal faith. It is dangerous to speculate one's self, in the slightest measure, away from the foundation of apostolic truth. A man wrests vital truth to his own desolation.

25. And this. Namely, the reality of abiding in the Son and Father; this union with them just spoken of. So Hackett. **Is the promise that he** (that is, Christ, who is the centre of thought in many verses back) **hath promised us.** When he was on earth. Union with Son and Father is the essence or principle of that which was promised—namely, the eternal life. **Even (*the*) eternal life** is in a sense appositional with 'the promise,' but in form (Greek) is attracted into the case of the intervening relative. In John 17: 3, the knowledge of the true God and Jesus Christ is substantially eternal life. But this knowledge *is union with its object.* "Oneness in will with God, and partaking of his nature, is itself eternal life." (Alford.) The eternal life is divine life, or spiritual life, the true life, or the life indeed (1 Tim. 6: 19, Greek text), something distinct from continuous natural existence which sinners, even devils, possess. One must carefully mark this distinction, that he be not entangled in the snare of materialism. Men who already possessed natural existence received the superadded gift of the life indeed. Eternal life is the life of the Spirit. One has this life the moment he believes. The interpretations given to eternal life by materialism and spiritual religion are irreconcilably different. The former makes it the mere carrying on of natural existence, so that notwithstanding death there is being afterwards; while the latter makes it another and new life, beginning the moment one believes, it may be long before death; something which does not make natural existence any more certain after death, but turns it into a blessing. Mere conscious existence, temporary or eternal, is not of itself necessarily a blessing. It may be a curse. The devils find it so. Lost men will find it so. Only the new life laid upon it can make it a blessing to one who has sinned. Christ did not die to purchase for us mere continuous conscious existence. He purchased for us a new life, able to turn conscious existence, otherwise a curse, into a blessing; an existence out of God, into a blissful one in God.

26. These things. That have preceded (see note on 1: 4) from ver. 18 onward, regarding the false teachers and their denial of the truth. **Have I written unto you concerning them that seduce you.** 'Seduce you' from the truth. Doing it as an occupation. It is the act of deceiving and causing to wander. John puts the faithful on their guard, and fortifies them by impressing them with the enormity of the antichristian error, and its logical outcome. He implies that there are aspects to the teaching or acting of errorists that are seductive, calculated to deceive, were it possible, the very elect. It has such a part of truth, or is so agreeable to the natural heart, or is accompanied with such professions of sincerity, or such appearance of amiability, or invites to such associations, or so flatters the vanity of intellectualism or singularity, that it is *adapted* to deceive; and the warning must be emphatic.

27. But the anointing which ye have received of him abideth in you. The Revised Version is more literal: *And as for you*, etc. See note on ver. 24. It vividly contrasts the apostle's trusted readers with the doctrinal seducers, and introduces the favorite testimony of the spiritual standing that made them as a rock against all error. 'The anointing.' Anointing-oil; emblematic name of the Holy Spirit. There must be a reason why here and in ver. 20, this particular name is given to the Spirit when his work is regarded as the source of the spiritual knowledge of Christians. Is that reason suggested in Rev. 3: 18? 'Which ye have received.' When

teach you: but as the same anointing teacheth you of all things, and is truth, and is no lie, and even as it hath taught you, ye shall adide in him.
28 And now, little children, abide in him; that, when

ye need not that any one teach you; but as his anointing teacheth you concerning all things, [1]and is true, and is no lie, and even as it taught you, [2]ye
28 abide in him. And now, *my* little children, abide

1 Or, *so it is true, and is no lie; and even as, &c.* ....2 Or, *abide ye.*

they were first consciously saved. This receiving is by the hearing of faith (Gal. 3: 2), and by obeying. (Acts 5: 32.) 'From him'—namely, Christ (2: 20), who has the Spirit to give to his people in fulfillment of one of his divine offices. The one ever present to the apostle's thought, the one about whom both error and faith chiefly revolved, the one running as a life-current in all the Epistle, needed only a pronoun by which to be recognized. 'Abideth in you.' It is no temporary gift. Once received, the Spirit abides in us, as do his graces. (1 Cor. 13: 13.) True, his *manifestations* in experience may be hid at times; but he himself remains an eternal possession. **And ye need not.** And so ye have no need. **That any man teach you.** There may be some peculiar meaning in the word 'that' (ἵνα), some sort of aim or purpose, as if a need of knowledge were *designed* to invite instruction; still it is simpler to take Winer's position, and regard the word 'that' here, with its verb, as used in place of the infinitive as found in Heb. 5: 12; Matt. 3: 14; 1 Thess. 1: 8, a usage beginning to appear in New Testament times, and now universally employed in the modern Greek. See John 2: 25; 16: 30; 18: 39. It is evident from Jer. 31: 33; John 6: 45; Heb. 8: 10; 1 John 2: 20, that there is a knowledge on the part of the regenerate—given by the Holy Spirit—which supersedes the necessity of external teachers. This knowledge relates to the nature of spiritual objects. It is qualitative and discriminative. The objects being presented, it knows the true through the Spirit. (1 Cor. 2: 11, 14.) The Spirit in us does not reveal new truth, but illumines, certifies, and leads into the old, and roots it in the convictions. And by this we are fortified against the novelties and errors of human wisdom. **But.** In contrast with '*need not.*' **As the same anointing.** The weight of criticism is altogether in favor of the words 'of him' (Revised Version "his") in place of 'the same': The anointing of him—that is, of Christ. And this rendering helps to carry the mind to Christ as the subject of the word 'hath taught' near the close of the verse, and the one meant by 'in him' at the very close. **Teacheth.** This work of the Spirit is continuous and ever present; while Christ taught (ἐδίδαξεν) once for all, and passed to heaven. If Christ teaches now, it is by the Spirit. **And is truth.** Or, better, *true.* Said of the Spirit. And if he be true, he is no lie (compare ver. 21), and his teaching is exclusive and binding—his teaching especially, that we should abide in Christ, for all that he is. **And even as it hath taught you.** The 'and' naturally introduces something additional to the Spirit's teaching; and the 'even as,' stronger than the simple "as" before given, naturally introduces something that backs up and makes more cogent the lesson coming from the Spirit's teaching. And what is so likely to be that something additional, and that something enforcing the Spirit's lesson, as a citing of Christ's own teaching of the same tenor and effect? Then the aorist tense of the word 'taught' (not, 'hath taught') points back to the definite historical act of some person, other than the Spirit, who is a constant working presence. And what so natural as to think here of the oral teaching of Christ, especially as he is brought into view at the opening of the sentence, and is surely referred to by the words **abide in him** at the close? And, to confirm all, there is the known record in John 15: 4, that he did teach his people this very duty, to abide in him. This teaching of Christ's own lips, we believe John recalls, to enforce the Spirit's teaching, as against the seduction of the antichrists. Our rendering of this difficult passage then is: *But as the anointing of him teaches you concerning all things, and is true and is not a lie, and even as he* (Christ himself) *taught you, abide* (μένετε, not the future μενεῖτε) *in him.*

28. And now denotes simple transition to a new phase of the matter of abiding in Christ. John had just urged it from the consideration that it was the Spirit's and the Lord's teaching. He now urges it from the consideration of the Lord's second coming. **Little children.** Humble, beloved, born of

he shall appear, we may have confidence, and not be
ashamed before him at his coming.
29 If ye know that he is righteous, ye know that
every one that doeth righteousness is born of him.

in him; that, if he shall be manifested, we may
have boldness, and not be ashamed [1] before him at
29 his [2] coming. If ye know that he is righteous, [3] ye
know that every one also that doeth righteousness
is begotten of him.

1 Gr. *from him*......2 Gr. *presence*......3 Or, *know ye*.

God. The very name an enforcement of spiritual obligations, and inspiring loving obedience. **Abide in him.** In Christ. Repeated from the close of the preceding verse, partly from the importance of the injunction, partly that the apostle may lay it upon the hearts of his dear ones as his own independent charge, but most of all for the sake of enforcing it with the new consideration of the approaching second advent. The certainty of our salvation is consistent with watchful caution and effort lest we be lost. None of the men in the ship (Acts 27: 22-24) shall be lost. Nevertheless, "except these (men) abide in the ship, ye cannot be saved." (27: 31.) God works the sure result through our free acting. Means as well as ends are of God's purpose. There is something wrong about an assurance that is careless. The one actually safe in Christ will try carefully to abide in him. **That when he** (Christ) **shall appear** (better, *if he be manifested*, at any time, as he will be some time), **we may have confidence** (or, *boldness*). The boldness is that childlike freedom, that perfect sense of justification, that up-looking spiritual assurance, which they have who are consciously in Christ, and which they will have under the greatest revelation, even that of the Lord coming in the air. (1 Thess. 4: 17.) **And not be ashamed** (shrink with shame) **before** (literally, *from*) **him**—that is, from Christ, the Judge. The expression 'from (ἀπὸ) him' implies a motion of the body; it may be an averting or hanging of the face, caused by the sense of shame belonging to conscious guilt. This feeling is the opposite of that boldness in the day of judgment (4: 17), cheering those united to Christ. **At his coming.** In his 'coming' or *presence* (παρουσία), when manifested at the last day. The important word occurs but once in all John's writings, though several times elsewhere in the New Testament.

29. If ye know (as a fact) **that he is righteous.** The previous context, which has suggested the idea of righteousness here, demands that the word 'he' should relate to Christ. It is the natural subject; and it brings us back to the very character of Christ with which the chapter opened: 'Jesus Christ (who is) righteous.' See note on 2: 1. This character of Christ is suggested by the boldness or shame felt by those who meet him at his second coming. These feelings imply the righteous attribute in him. Besides, righteousness is always thought of as a kind of omnipresence at the second advent. Ver. 28 suggests the opening declaration of ver. 29. Of course, if 'he' refers to Christ, 'of him' at the close most naturally has the same reference. And why may not the believer be said to be born or begotten of Christ? Strictly, it is the Holy Spirit who is the agent in regeneration, and it is Christ who works in the work of the Spirit as much and as truly as it is the Father. [In 1 Cor. 4: 15 Paul says: "For in Christ Jesus"—that is, in the power of Christ Jesus exercised doubtless by the Holy Spirit—"I begat you through the gospel"—a passage confirming the view of the author.—A. H.] **Ye know** (experimentally) **that every one that doeth righteousness is born** (or *begotten*) **of him.** The doing of righteousness, as a tree bears fruit and as a continuous activity, is intimately connected with abiding in Christ. It is doing as Christ the righteous one does. It is acting out the same nature and life. It is the proof of kinship, of the new birth. And they who have this relationship with Christ will find their family likeness to him perfected as they meet him at the final day (3: 2), and will not be ashamed. It is 3: 2 that completes the thought of this verse, and brings it up into relation with the searching *parousia* noticed in the preceding verse. Spiritual kinship in the new birth guarantees moral and spiritual likeness, and such likeness will produce the home feeling before the manifested Christ.

CHAPTER III.

BEHOLD, what manner of love the Father hath bestowed upon us, that we should be called the sons

1 Behold what manner of love the Father hath bestowed upon us, that we should be called children

Ch. 3: 1-3. THE CHILD OF GRACE, CHERISHING A HOPE OF GLORY, PURIFIES HIMSELF.

The Christ-nature as a nature of righteousness, taught in 2: 29, suggests much of the thought of this new chaper. "Verse 29 is the conclusion of the preceding part: but it is in such a manner, that it is the organic germ out of which the following part is developed." (Ebrard.) Again and again, by the tender epithet of "little children," John has reminded his faithful readers of their new-birth relation to God. But in 2: 29 he has brought this position of Christians into more distinct view, and this it is—this sonship, or rather divine *childship* of the believer—which calls forth the admiring exclamation, with which the present section opens.

1. Behold. See, all of you. Let it fill, for the moment, all your thought. Let it stand out before the mind as a lofty object before the natural eyes. **What manner of love.** What peculiar kind of love, and how great love. The quality and the degree of the divine grace in the case are both marked. As to its kind, there was nothing like it among men. As to its degree, it was without measure and beyond expression. Such is that love that lies behind all the power and privilege of salvation. (John 3: 16; Rom. 5: 8; Titus 3: 4; 1 John 4: 10.) The tree of life in any soul is rooted in the love of God. The river of life has its fountain in the bosom of God.[1] **The Father hath bestowed upon us**—literally, *given to us.* The name is suggested by the particular grace relating to sonship, and uttered with a personal sense of the filial relation. By the giving of love (James 4: 6) is meant the bestowal of it in its expression and effect. Doubtless this gift of love connects itself in the writer's mind with the gift of Christ. **That we should be called the sons of God.** Better, *children of God;* since the term points not only to relation, privilege, or honor, but to a nature received by the divine begetting. Every true Christian is one whom God has begotten; he has been made a partaker of the divine nature; hence his spiritual childhood. The word 'that' (ἵνα, *in order that*) brings forward the purpose, or designed effect, of the wonderful love bestowed. 'Should be called,' by whom? By God himself, and by all intelligent beings in heaven or earth, who sympathize in God's judgment. It is by the Father primarily that one is named his child. It is a divine title. It implies divine recognition, and adoption. To be called thus a child of God is the public acknowledgment of the relation instituted in regeneration. Nor will God at any time disown the relation. To confess it is of his love and delight. As an earthly child better realizes and rejoices in it when an honored parent fondly recognizes him as his child, so the Christian better realizes and prizes his divine child-relation when assured that the Father owns it. John counts it a great thing that such as we should receive this divine name. Here is an humble sense of his own, and his brethren's, ill deservings, which enhances the wonder of their recognition by God himself as his children. The saved sinner feels the unworthiest of all. (1 Tim. 1: 15.) Divine love touching a sinner and lifting him to an acknowledged place in the divine family! Evidently our apostle views the title, 'children of God,' as peculiar and distinctive, and belonging to only a portion of mankind. A certain class of religionists speak of all as the children of God. There is a remote sense in which all are children of God—that is, in virtue of creation. But this is rarely alluded to in the Bible. The true sonship is by the new birth, and spiritual kinship with Christ. We are children of God in virtue of regeneration, and union with Christ—union with him so as to stand in his relation, and receive his very name. The fatherhood of God is to be defined

[[1] Huther remarks that "ποταπός (a later form of ποδαπός, properly=whence), never used in the New Testament for a direct question, is not strictly=*quantus*, but=*qualis* (compare Luke 1: 29; 2 Peter 3: 11), but is often used as an expression of wonder at something specially glorious (compare Matt. 8: 27; Mark 13: 1; Luke 7: 39), so that the meaning of *qualis* plays over into that of *quantus*. So here."—A. H.]

of God: therefore the world knoweth us not, because it knew him not.
2 Beloved, now are we the sons of God, and it doth not yet appear what we shall be: but we know that, when he shall appear, we shall be like him; for we shall see him as he is.

of God: and *such* we are. For this cause the world
2 knoweth us not, because it knew him not. Beloved,
now are we children of God, and it is not yet made
manifest what we shall be. We know that, if
[1] he shall be manifested, we shall like him; for we
3 shall see him even as he is. And every one that hath

[1] Or, *it*.

in this relation. God is pre-eminently the Father of Christ, and of those in him. "And (*such*) we are." (Rev. Ver.) This clause, inserted by the best text, asserts the reality of the childship, justifying the name, and meeting a possible cavil. **Therefore the world knoweth us not.** On this account. Since we are children of God by a new nature, raised into a new sphere of life, endowed with the principles and attributes of a new race, clothed with traits and privileges appropriate to this higher relation—for this cause the world does not know us. The world has some general judgment of the Christian by his outward fruits. But the new life within, the new spiritual nature, which makes one a child of God, the world does not know. It has never experienced it. It is a spiritual thing, and must be spiritually discerned. The world has no way of discerning between a natural amiability and a grace of the Spirit. **Because it knew him not**—namely, Christ, when he was on earth. The person and the fact were too well known to require the name to be given. The inability of the world to discern the Christian's nature was manifest in men's treatment of Christ himself. (John 1:5, 10; 16:3; 1 Cor. 2:8.) The world could not see that in Christ which did most to make him what he was, and so rejected him. And if we have received any part of Christ's nature, we need not expect any better appreciation. A people to a great extent not understood must we be. We should count the cost, in making friends with Christ. (4:17; Matt. 10:25; John 15:19.)

2. Beloved. Not appreciated by the world, yet known and appreciated. The epithet means (1) loved by God and fellow-Christians, (2) possessed by the love-grace, (3) impliedly, lovable. **Now.** Temporal, not logical. Emphatic, in contrast with the 'not yet' which follows. Though esteemed as earthen pitchers (Lam. 4:2), yet are believers even now the precious sons of Zion comparable to fine gold. Though earthly eyes see it not, they are already children of God, allied to him in a new nature. **And it doth not yet appear** (*it is not yet made manifest*) **what we shall be.** What we shall be is no uncertainty, but it is not yet manifested. Our being already God's children is the guaranty of the fullest perfection, which some time will be manifested to all beings. What God sees inwardly shall as plainly be seen outwardly. The light within must shine out, as Christ was transfigured. What the divine childship involves must be evolved; the latent must become patent. **We know.** As a fact (οἴδαμεν). How much John says about *knowing!* In the presence of Christian revelation and experience, we do not conjecture: we know. The connective **but** (δὲ) is erased in the critical text, and the new sentence begins with perfect independence. **That when he shall appear** (or, *if he shall be manifested*). The subject seems to be, on the whole, Christ, and not the 'what we shall be' of the preceding sentence. That our verb should have a personal subject best accords with the mention of 'him' in the next clause; and that this personal subject is Christ is shown in 2:28. Compare Col. 3:4; Phil. 3:20, 21. The manifestation of Christ and all his people is to be at his second coming, in the end of the world. **We shall be like him**—namely, Christ, who is our pattern. The likeness (see Rom. 8:29) will be in the unfolded spiritual nature and in the resurrection body—in other words, in the manifested glory of the risen and perfect human nature. Until that event, our life is hid with Christ. (Col. 3:3.) Even through the state between death and the resurrection, though we shall be with the Lord, we shall not have reached the state of glorious manifestation, and that likeness to Christ which our passage anticipates. **For** or, *because* **we shall see him as he is.** (Gen. 22:14.) The one referred to is plainly Christ; but the relation of the sentence to the preceding context is difficult to decide. It certainly states the reason (ὅτι) for something. Is it (1) the reason for the likeness? Is the final vision of the glorified Jesus instrumental in bringing about the likeness to

3 And every man that hath this hope in him purifieth himself, even as he is pure.
4 Whosoever committeth sin transgresseth also the law: for sin is the transgression of the law.

this hope *set* on him purifieth himself, even as he is
4 pure. Every one that doeth sin doeth also lawlessness:
5 and sin is lawlessness. And ye know that he was

him, according to the principle involved in 2 Cor. 3: 18? Does John state this in our present sentence? Or (2) is it the statement of an evidential reason? In other words, the reason why in the last day we shall know that we are like Christ, or why now we may have confidence that the full likeness shall be? It is certain that we are to see him just as he is; that is proof that we shall have already become like him, since a perfect likeness is necessary to a perfect vision. Or (3) is our sentence a statement confirming the fact supposed in the words 'if he should be manifested'? In other words, does it relate to the protasis rather than the apodosis of the preceding sentence? And that he will be manifested is certain, because we are surely to see him, even just as he is, and that involves his literal manifestation. Either of these three explanations is plausible, and easily understood. Probably, in the present instance, we must serve the reader by clearly stating them, without making an absolute decision for one of them. We know that (1) is the more common interpretation, but the thought is rather forced and refined, the philosophy a little remote. Besides, it implies an order in the transformation at and following the resurrection not otherwise to be thought of. For it implies that the elect will be raised up in some unnamed moral and physical form, then get a vision of Christ, and then, upon that, be further transformed into his full likeness. It is also more probable that the likeness should precede the seeing and appreciating of Christ, and be necessary to it (Ps. 17: 15), as (2) implies. As for (3), it is new, but is at least worth considering.

3. And every man that hath this hope in (literally, *upon* ἐπί) **him.** That is, upon Christ, the ground on which the hope rests; the hope, namely, of resurrection glory and likeness to Christ. **Purifieth himself.** Here in this world, and as an on-going thing. The confidence of the glorious end, modeled to us in Christ, will lead those who feel it now to imitate him. We tend to become like that which we hope for. **Even as he** (ἐκεῖνος) **is pure.** The demonstrative 'he,' *that one*, refers back to the pronoun 'him' (αὐτῷ), and hence to Christ. The model of the purity is complete.

4-9. RIGHTEOUSNESS, AND NOT SIN, IS THE GRAND CHARACTERISTIC OF THE REGENERATE.

Sin is incompatible with birth from God. John had just stated that he who hopes for Christ-likeness at the resurrection will now seek to copy him in holy living. This leads him to present the true moral ideal of the Christian, which he does in explicit language, with the aid of those spherical and mutually exclusive conceptions so common to this writer. He implies that this ideal is a constant argument against sinning, a prevailing motive to personal holiness.

4. Whosoever committeth sin. In contrast with the one seeking purity. It is the doer of sin. That is his nature and character, as the evil tree bearing evil fruit. He lives in the sphere of sin. **Transgresseth also the law**—literally, *doeth lawlessness*, that which is a deviation from law (ἀνομία). The sinning may be of any sort, small or great, of the heart or of the life; it is not merely something bad in itself; it is also in every instance a transgressing of God's law, a violation of his personal will, an affront to God himself. A man may plead that he is only a little sinner; that though he fails towards God he does his duty by his fellows, and so lull his conscience. But John will not let a man rest there. He declares that the doer of any sin is a transgressor of law, a criminal in the eyes of God. We are under the divine government, and it is one of omnipresent law; and the sinner, of whatsoever sort or dimensions, is a rebel against it. Both the offense and the rightful condemnation are thus exposed. **For sin is the transgression of the law.** The violation of the will of God. (Ps. 51: 4.) What better definition of sin? Both subject and predicate in the Greek have the article. "Each term being thus an abstract or universal, the resulting statement is that sin and breach of the law are identical to the full extent of each." (T. S. Green, "New Testament Gram.," p. 36.) [Would it not then

5 And ye know that he was manifested to take away our sins; and in him is no sin.

manifested to [1]take away sins; and in him is no sin.
6 Whosoever abideth in him sinneth not: whosoever

[1] Or, *bear sins.*

be better to omit the article before "transgression" as well as before "sin" in translating, thus: *Sin is transgression of law?*—A. H.] All sin is law-breaking. The Christian by subtle sophistry may think a sin is not for him as criminal as it would be for another. Our apostle rebukes and corrects this by declaring all sin to be against the will and nature of God. Another might imbibe the antinomian idea that, having been saved by Christ, he is out of the pale of law, and cannot be controlled or judged by it. John dissipates this fancy. He says that any defect or deflection from the right is transgression of law in the saved man as well as in others. The law searches and tries every man. It is the measure of character. And this transgression of law is the transgression of the whole law considered as a unity (James 2: 10), as it is the violation of the one will of God, and touches the one God. Christ was God's law embodied. In him we can see that the law is holy, just, and good; is spiritual, reaching the thoughts and feelings of the heart; applies not merely to outward matters, but to all the inward moral life. Hence, every failure to reach the pure spirit of Christ may be known as the transgression of law.

5. And ye know (the fact, hence οἴδατε) **that he** (*that one*, Christ) **was manifested** (*in the flesh*) **to take away our sins.** The 'our' of the Common Version is not in the now accepted text. The very statement that Christ was 'manifested' implies his pre-existence. (John 8: 58.) But why did he come in the flesh? It was 'to take away our' ('our' is not in the Greek) 'sins'—to *lift up and bear away* (ἄρῃ) the sins of men (Matt. 1: 21; John 1: 29; Heb. 9: 28; 1 Peter 2: 24) by his sacrifice as the Lamb of God. [See a careful article in the Bibliotheca Sacra, Vol. 32, p. 475 seq., on "The New Testament View of Christ as Bearing Sin," by Rev. W. H. Cobb.—A. H.] All 'sins' (plural) need atonement, and this confirms what had been just said of their criminality; and that there is atonement inspires hope in the midst of the dark array of sins which the apostle has made. The deep conviction properly awakened by ver. 4 is followed by the great salvation of ver. 5. Sin, sin, then, was the dreadful occasion of Christ's coming in the flesh. Our sins called him here. These tried and oppressed his soul. These nailed him to the cross. These led him to provide for pardon and moral purification by the suffering of death. It would seem from the general context that John's phrase, 'to take away sins' has a double meaning—namely, pardon and purifying. Christ's death for sinners provided both. Thereby the penalty of sin was borne, and we, repenting, are freed from guilt; thereby the Holy Spirit is procured, and we, appropriating that agent, are purified. And the whole work is one. For we are pardoned, not that we may go on sinning, but that we may more surely have a holy character. The manifested Christ is the source, not only of pardon, but of moral purification; and the latter because of the former. It is all embraced in the idea of taking away sins. (1 Peter 2: 24.) Sanctification follows justification as fruit follows blossom. Moral fruit comes out of the legal transaction. A religion that does not purify does not pardon. Christ's advent looked to the nature of sin as well as the guilt of sin. The object of Christ's manifestation in the flesh being thus comprehensive, John wishes to know if it is being accomplished in his brethren. If they are not aiming at the same thing that Christ came for, how are they in sympathy with him? How can they claim salvation while indifferent about its moral effects? If Christ thought enough of sins to come from heaven and die on account of them, shall we think lightly of them? can we lightly live in them? The passage terribly arouses the slumbering conscience of the careless religious professor. **And in him is no sin.** The complete moral purity of Christ is here recalled for several reasons: 1. To show that he was prepared in character to be a sin-bearer for others; 2. To suggest that he would specially desire the purity of his people; 3. To give them a strong motive to this in his own example and position with regard to sin; 4. To prepare the way for the doctrine of the next verse.

6. Christ came to get sin out of the way;

6 Whosoever abideth in him sinneth not: whosoever sinneth hath not seen him, neither known him.
7 Little children, let no man deceive you: he that
doeth righteousness is righteous, even as he is righteous.
8 He that committeth sin is of the devil; for the

sinneth hath not seen him, neither [1]knoweth him.
7 *My* little children, let no man lead you astray: he
that doeth righteousness is righteous, even as he is
8 righteous: he that doeth sin is of the devil; for the

1 Or, *hath known.*

not only so, he stood apart from sin in his own character. And this last assertion prepares for the words that follow. **Whosoever abideth in him sinneth not.** The abiding in Christ is the state of vital union with him. If in him there is no sin, then those absolutely united to him and identified with him must partake of his sinless character, and be like him in that respect. What! do they not sin at all? Is the Christian a sinless being? If John's reasoning means the sinlessness of any Christians, it means the sinlessness of all who in their conversion have entered into union with Christ, and their sinlessness during all the period of salvation. But this contradicts 1: 8 and that progressive work of purification which the Christian in 3: 3 is said to carry on. It contradicts our conscious life. Now, what is the interpretation of John's language? We answer by saying that in this and similar cases he states an ideal or principle. He presents what the divine union involves in its fullness, that which will be when our union with Christ shall be developed in experience and actual life to its normal and perfected state. Abiding in Christ in its fulfilled degree will involve a partaking in full of the holiness of Christ. This ideal had not yet been fully reached by John and his brethren, though the union had richly commenced and was going on. But he looks forward to their perfected union with the Lord, and predicates of it complete purity; nay, he even speaks of it as if it were present, since the beginning in all grace involves the ending, the germ the full unfolding; as the New Testament calls every Christian a saint, not because he has reached that ideal, but with reference to the perfection which is yet to be. John gives us the *law*, or *principle*, of union with Christ. Purity characterizes this union; and so far as the union is realized and fulfilled, so far there will be purity, until the ideal becomes fully real, and then, by the very law of the union, there will be utter sinlessness. The union is a holy principle, and the more it is developed the more it bears personal holiness with it. The Christian, therefore, by the very law of his union with Christ, is one who is reaching on to moral purity; and if not approaching the ideal, he may doubt his spiritual state. Purity is the law, the tendency, of divine union. **Whosoever sinneth hath not seen him** (Christ), **neither known him.** Has not had either a *vision* of him, or an *experience* of him; is now in a state of spiritual blindness and ignorance. "The Greek perfect denotes an abiding present effect resting on an event in the past. In the Greek perfect the *present* predominates." (Alford.) John states antithetically a truth implied in the former part of the verse—a truth that comes out from the mutual exclusiveness of the sin character and the Christ character. John states here the law, or tendency, of the sin character. He who sins as his law, the on-going, developing law of his life, knows nothing of the saving vision or purifying knowledge of Christ. Sin is blinding. Sin is the foe of divine fellowship. If this be the total effect in the unregenerate, is it not to the Christian dust in his spiritual sight and a palsy in his spiritual love?

7. Little children. An appeal of affection and a reminder of the spiritual standing of those addressed. **Let no man deceive you.** Lead you astray, or cause you to wander. If little children, they need caution against the wiles of false teachers, as sheep need guarding against devouring beasts. False teachers, antichrists, had already appeared, and it would seem that some of them were teaching that one might be a Christian, and so belong to the class of the righteous, yet go on sinning as before, without condemnation. "Be not deceived," says the apostle, "with such teaching. Know that if one is a Christian he is of the class of the righteous, and his doing, the fruit of his life, will agree with this fact. He will reflect Christ, who, righteous himself, was for that reason a doer of righteousness. The being proves itself in the doing. The good tree brings forth good fruit."

8. He that committeth (or *doeth*) **sin.** Defined as in the note on ver. 4. The sin

devil sinneth from the beginning. For this purpose the Son of God was manifested, that he might destroy the works of the devil.
9 Whosoever is born of God doth not commit sin; for his seed remaineth in him: and he cannot sin, because he is born of God.

devil sinneth from the beginning. To this end
was the Son of God manifested, that he might de-
9 stroy the works of the devil. Whosoever is begot-
ten of God doeth no sin, because his seed abideth
in him: and he cannot sin, because he is begotten
10 of God. In this the children of God are manifest,

doer is here contrasted with the righteous doer of the preceding verse, as to his ideal likeness and relationship. **Is of the devil.** Who, with this verse and ver. 10 in mind, can doubt the personality of the devil? And why doubt it any more than that of an angel? What is gained, in any interest of reason or religion, by doubting it? The devil is the ideal, the fully developed, sinner. The sinning man finds the goal to which he is tending, the type to which he is approximating, the same moral nature of which he has partaken, in the devil. There is his kinship. To be of the devil is to have his moral likeness, and the same law of sin. In this sense the sinner on earth is a child, and the devil a father. (John 8: 44; Acts 13: 10.) **From the beginning.** Of human history, when there was man to slay morally. (John 8: 44.) **For this purpose** (or *to this end*). The purpose is stated in the last part of the sentence. **The Son of God was manifested.** In his total earthly career, including his death. (Heb. 2: 14.) 'The Son of God,' begotten through the Holy Spirit. (Luke 1: 35.) A historical, not a metaphysical name. **That he might destroy the works of the devil.** "Those works which he incites men to perform" (Hackett)—namely, sins. These Christ destroys (λύσῃ), dissolves by his death (Heb. 9: 26) and his Spirit (Rom. 8: 13), and by weakening Satan himself. (Gen. 3: 15.) Christ is the opposite of the devil in character and works. Whom will the believer take sides with? Will he make that his law which Christ came to destroy?

9. Whosoever (that is, *every one*) **is born of** (ἐκ) **God.** And (perfect participle) now possesses the new-birth nature. [It might be translated, "Every one who has been born of God."—A. H.] **Doth not commit** (or *do*) **sin.** Does not do it (present and continuous tense) as the law of his life, as the ideal tendency of his being; does not belong to the sin sphere. He belongs rather to the sphere of light, having God's nature through the new birth. The states of being begotten of God, and of sin, are viewed as mutually exclusive. This is the normal, ideal fact. "And John sets up the ideal as the true reality." (Godet.) See explanation of ver. 6. **For** (or *because*) **his** (God's) **seed abideth in him**—that is, in the one born of God. The seed (sperm) is the word of God quickened in the heart by the Holy Spirit, and so made the principle of regeneration. (1 Peter 1: 23; James 1: 18; John 5: 38.) It is holy as God is holy; and as seed it germinates and expands, filling the being, making real the holy ideal. [It is by no means certain that the expression 'his seed' (σπέρμα αὐτοῦ) means "the word of God." Many interpreters think it means the Spirit of God; others think it is the new disposition generated by the Spirit. This new disposition, implanted by the gracious influence of the Spirit, is however called into action by the light of divine truth, and appears to the eye of consciousness as faith, love, hope, etc. "The good seed are the children of the kingdom; but the tares are the children of the wicked one." (Matt. 13: 38.) The figure is not precisely the same in this parable as in the verse before us; but it favors the view that the word 'seed' has reference to the vital principle, or holy disposition imparted to the soul, rather than to Christian truth—a more objective reality. How can truth be vitalized, made to germinate?—A. H.] **And he cannot sin.** To sin, in the sense explained at the opening of the verse. **Because he is** (literally, *has been*) **born of God.** And it is as impossible (ού δύναται) for him to sin, in the sense explained, as it is for the nature of God to sin. And as the nature of God in us abides and grows, as the child becomes the man, the old sin nature is sloughed off, and absolute holiness is reached. The divine germ and potency are the law, and what is law must be fulfilled.

10 18. THAT RIGHTEOUSNESS WHICH DISTINGUISHES THE CHILDREN OF GOD FROM THE CHILDREN OF THE DEVIL INCLUDES, IN PARTICULAR, LOVE OF THE BRETHREN, WHICH LOVE MUST BE PRACTICAL AS WELL AS PROFESSIONAL

We are impressed with the explicit, direct, and positive nature of the apostle's statements

10 In this the children of God are manifest, and the children of the devil: whosoever doeth not righteousness is not of God, neither he that loveth not his brother.
11 For this is the message that ye heard from the beginning, that we should love one another.
12 Not as Cain, *who* was of that wicked one, and slew his brother. And wherefore slew he him? Because his own works were evil, and his brother's righteous.

and the children of the devil: whosoever doeth not
righteousness is not of God, neither he that loveth
11 not his brother. For this is the message which
ye heard from the beginning, that we should
12 love one another: not as Cain was of the evil
one, and slew his brother. And wherefore slew
he him? Because his works were evil, and his
brother's righteous.

under this section. There is no such thing here as a halting or timid utterance; no disposition to cover the edge of truth, in order to spare the feelings of any who cannot stand the gospel tests. Our heading of the present section has sufficiently indicated its outgrowth from the preceding section.

10. In this. In this evidencing fact. **The children of God are manifest, and the children of the devil.** 'Are manifest' to all who will look into the matter, and reflect upon it. One might say to John, "You have divided the world into these two classes, the one bearing in their soul the image of God, the other the image of the devil. They are mixed up together; how shall they be distinguished? By what test are they 'manifest'?" By this criterion, says John, which follows: **Whosoever doeth not righteousness is not of God, neither he that loveth not his brother.** A very plain, short rule. Doing righteousness is doing that which likens us to Christ. See 2: 29 and note. The child of God will do this righteousness naturally. To further define this righteousness John mentions brotherly love as a part of it and co-ordinates it with it. An important part of practical righteousness is this love, which is so essential that he who lacks it cannot be a Christian. (John 13: 35.) It is that which shows what the hidden child-nature is. It is pre-eminently the revealing grace. Our verse, then, tends to unfold what practical righteousness is, and fairly introduces us to the subject of brotherly love, as marking the new nature.

11. For introduces proof of the position that the righteousness of brotherly love must distinguish God's children. It was one of the first things taught by the gospel, that Christ's people should love one another, that the family of God should have the family grace. It is therefore that manifestation which we expect to find distinguishing the children of God from the children of the devil. For explanation of **beginning,** see on 2: 7, and of **love one another,** see on 2: 8. This love is not love to all men, but is that which springs out of our relationship as children of one Father, and such as Christ had for his own (John 13: 34); it is involved in the kinship of nature. **That** (ἵνα). "Purpose and purport." (Alford.) "Declarative." (Hackett.)

12. Not as Cain, who was of that wicked one, and slew his brother. The words, *and so be,* supplied at the beginning of the sentence, would complete the sense, and connect it with the last words of ver. 11: "should love one another and so be not like wicked Cain." But the brief form in the text is in the interest of vividness and force. Compare John 6: 58, for construction. The example of Cain strikingly illustrates the love-precept by way of contrast. He wickedly violated the brotherly relation. Instead of loving his brother, he hated and slew him, acting out the nature of Satan, who was a murderer from the beginning. His deed showed what his nature was, with whom allied. Instead of making a sacrifice of love for his own brother, Cain took that brother and sacrificed him to his god, the devil. If Christians will not love another, they violate their assumed brotherly relation, and repeat the spirit of Cain and the devil. What a tell-tale mirror for an unloving Christian to look into. [The Revised Version translates: *not as Cain was of the evil one,* etc. The sense would then be, "that we should love one another, not being (of the evil one) as Cain was of the evil one, etc.—A. H.] **And wherefore** (χάριν τίνος). On account of what. **Because his own works were evil.** (Omit the word 'own,' for which there is nothing in the original.) Morally evil, hence wicked; bearing the nature of the wicked one. What is meant by the 'works' (ἔργα) of the two brothers? The term is *plural* as related to each of them, and therefore suggests something more than the one work of each just preceding the murder. The customary deeds, the manner of life, the opposite moral characters, of the two men, are meant. The act of

13 Marvel not, my brethren, if the world hate you.
14 We know that we have passed from death unto life, because we love the brethren. He that loveth not *his* brother abideth in death.
15 Whosoever hateth his brother is a murderer: and ye know that no murderer hath eternal life abiding in him.

13 Marvel not, brethren, if the world hateth you.
14 We know that we have passed out of death into
life, because we love the brethren. He that loveth
15 not abideth in death. Whosoever hateth his brother
is a murderer: and ye know that no murderer hath
16 eternal life abiding in him. Hereby know we

murder on Cain's part was no accident of his moral life. It had a reason in the natural character, the habitual deeds, of the heart. It was the fruit of an evil tree. Moreover, it was the outcome of a heart in contrariety to a righteous heart such as Abel's was. The evil nature is in antipathy to the righteous nature. It does not love it, is averse to it, envies it, hates it, even as Satan's nature antagonizes God's nature. The carnal mind is enmity against God and whoever is like God. This is John's deep philosophy of the murder.

13. Marvel not. A negative command in the present looks to the discontinuance of an act. In John's conception, his readers had begun to wonder. **My brethren.** Omit the 'my' of the Common Version. The love-relation of those addressed is recognized, and their distinction from those who hate. **If the world hate** (*hateth*, Revised Version) **you.** 'If' with the indicative shows that the hypothesis is a reality. The world does hate you. Do not marvel. For you see, as in the case of Cain and Abel, that the world-nature and the Christian nature are contrary. This explains it. "Because ye are not of the world, . . . therefore the world hateth you." (John 15: 19.) The very principle of the new nature which binds Christians to each other is an occasion of repulsion to the world. In referring his readers to the hatred they have from the world, he affords them, 1. A further example of the principle of opposition between the seed of God and the seed of the devil; 2. A motive for them to love each other the more. Hatred, want of sympathy, from the world, should draw them to each other the more closely, as the cold blast of winter makes the children of the family press to each other's warmth.

14. We. Emphatic, as set over against the world. **Know.** As a fact (οἴδαμεν). **That we have passed.** And are still in the state thus reached. **From death unto** (that is, *out of death into*) **life.** This life is the new life, the life of the Spirit, the eternal life, the divine life. The death is the state opposite; not of non-existence, for they existed while unregenerate; but of separation from the true life; in the darkness outside of God's nature of light. What a change, then, is that from death to life! **Because we love the brethren.** Members of the spiritual family. The love is the new life in action, and the sure proof that the life is present. (Ver. 10, 11.) After the severe testing of the preceding verses, the assurance of these words would be most comforting. And how many self-distrusting souls of trembling faith in all the gospel times have by them been helped to the assuring evidence of their regeneration. They find in their hearts that they feel a drawing to Christians, which they do not feel towards the society of the world, a delightful love for them, though poor, or marred, or imperfect, a peculiar pleasure in being where they congregate, relishing their exercises and enjoying their fellowship, and this tells them, and manifests to all (John 13: 35), that in them is that new nature which allies them with God and all his people. **He that loveth not his brother abideth in death.** 'His brother' does not belong to the approved text. The absence of spiritual love from the character, which of course includes love of the brethren, is the sure sign of still abiding in death, where all men are by nature. The unloving heart has never passed over from the death state. If a child of God is no more to us than anybody else; if the society of the Church is no more to us than the society of the world; if God's love does not work consciously in us and have its willing response—we are simply not converted.

15. Whosoever hateth his brother. Hatred soon comes of not loving; it is of the same root and kind, only in a more positive form. The negative state is by no means a neutral state. The heart that does not love has the seeds of positive hatred, which will start up when occasion comes. This hatred, however hidden, is essential murder, man-killing (ἀνθρωποκτόνος). It is that germ whence

16 Hereby perceive we the love *of God*, because he laid down his life for us: and we ought to lay down *our* lives for the brethren.

17 But whoso hath this world's good, and seeth his brother have need, and shutteth up his bowels *of compassion* from him, how dwelleth the love of God in him?

18 My little children, let us not love in word neither in tongue; but in deed and in truth.

love, because he laid down his life for us: and we
17 ought to lay down our lives for the brethren. But
whoso hath the world's goods, and beholdeth his
brother in need, and shutteth up his compassion
from him, how doth the love of God abide in him?
18 *My* little children, let us not love in word, neither
19 with the tongue; but in deed and truth. Hereby

all murder comes. He who looks on the heart sees there embryonic and responsible murder. The private malice, the secret grudge, the throbbing vengeance, the envy cherished in the heart, is murderous in its tendency. It is that from which Cain's murder sprang. The principal part of sin is in the heart. (Mat. 15: 19.) The present participle "hating" (translated 'hateth') probably suggests a hate which is a principle, something kept up and cherished. A good Christian may fall into the temptation temporarily, and still have the principle of eternal life abiding in him. But he will not cherish the evil feeling. He will cast it away, as a man will kick off the snare that has begun to entangle his feet. He will cry, 'O Lord, pardon my murder.' And God will pardon and save.

16. Hereby (or, *in this*)—namely, that Christ laid down his life for us. **Perceive** (or, *know*) **we the love.** (The sense is best given by omitting the article before love, as in the Revised Version.) 'Know' it sympathetically, spiritually, as something that has touched us, and affected us. Know what it is (4: 10), how great it is, how much it will move us to sacrifice for its dear object. **Because he** (ἐκεῖνος, *that one*, ever present to the thought of the apostle) **laid down his life.** For the usage, in case of this peculiar expression, see John 10: 11, 15 17, 18. It means a voluntary self-sacrifice. It expresses not only the extent of the sacrifice, but the absolute voluntariness of it. Laying down one's life is the same as giving one's self. (Gal. 2: 20; Eph. 5: 2.) And in Christ's case it is the action of the very highest love. (Eph. 5: 2, 25.) **For us.** In our behalf; for our good. And for us while we were yet sinners. (Rom. 5: 8.) **And we** (emphatic, we the followers of Christ) **ought.** Are under obligation to him who has planted divine love in us, and has appointed the relation between love and sacrifice for its object, and has exemplified it to us in him whom we follow. **To lay down our lives for the brethren.** If needful; if their true good shall require it. This is love in practical action. It is love's proof. (John 15: 13.) We must love each other, therefore, not only at convenience, but at cost, even to the giving of ourselves. Love is the giving of self.

17. But. Contrast the above law of love with a certain example. **Whoso hath** (a supposed case) **this** (literally, *the*) **world's good** (or, *goods*), **and seeth** (or, *beholdeth*) **his brother have need, and shutteth up his bowels of compassion from him** (not giving his pity, or his goods, much less his life, as required in ver. 16), **how dwelleth the love of God in him?** How is the true abiding element or principle of love in him? "It is put as a wondering question which challenges in vain a satisfactory answer.". (Hackett.) It is an argument, a question, from the greater to the less. If, not laying down his life for the good of his brother, he cannot even pity him or give him alms, how much Christly love can there be in him?

18. My little children. Omit 'my.' See explanation at 2: 1, 12, 13, 18. 28. **Let us not love in word, neither in tongue.** Better, *with the tongue*. The last term has the article in the best text. Word and the tongue are mere instruments of profession. Do not love by these only; by profession only. The love of the professed brother described in the preceding verse was only profession and talk. Let not yours be so. **But** (on the contrary, let it be) **in deed and in truth.** (1 Peter 1: 22, 23.) In the element of these. In actual doing, and in the way of God's truth in the case. How fittingly, how forcibly, this exhortation closes the searching discussion of the section! How much in the manner and spirit of the aged John, as we think of him! The love-exhortation was his most ready word, and his ministry uttered it most affectionately to the very end. Godet. "Com. on John," Vol. I., p. 61. Nor has the sound of that appeal yet died away, or its influence on renewed hearts.

19 And hereby we know that we are of the truth, and shall assure our hearts before him.
20 For if our heart condemn us, God is greater than our heart, and knoweth all things.

shall we know that we are of the truth, and shall
20 [1]assure our heart [2]before him: because if our heart
condemn us, God is greater than our heart, and
21 knoweth all things. Beloved, if our heart con-

1 Gr. *persuade*......2 Or, *before him, whereinsoever our heart condemn us; because God, &c.*

19-24. THE EXERCISE OF BROTHERLY LOVE IS ATTENDED BY AN ASSURANCE OF OUR CHRISTIAN STATE, BY A PEACEFULNESS OF CONSCIENCE, BY EFFECTUAL PRAYER, AND BY ABIDING FELLOWSHIP AND UNION WITH HIM WHO GAVE THE COMMANDMENTS, AND WHO GIVES US THE SPIRIT.

19. And hereby (literally, *in this*). Connection with the preceding verse is close. The loving of our brethren in deed and truth, so loving them as to endure self-denial for their sakes, is referred to as that, in the presence or exercise of which, not on the ground of which, we realize other great spiritual blessings. **We know.** The verb is future to the fulfilled condition, and also expresses certainty. Translate, *we shall* know (experimentally) **that we are of the truth,** of one nature with the truth, as if born of it. To be of the truth is more than to be truthful or true men. It is to be in a state of spiritual affinity with the truth of God as it is in Jesus, and including him. It is to be of the light of God (sons of light. John 12: 36), the reflection of his own nature. Spiritual attainments do not come single. If we have brotherly love, we have much with it. It brings other experiences with it; and one of these is the consciousness that we are neither deceivers nor self-deceived, that we belong to the spiritual sphere, that we are true Christians. **Before him.** Before God. (Ver. 20.) In his very sight. Even before the searching eye of his holiness. The position of the expression in the Greek suggests emphasis. The judgment day does not seem to be referred to as the day of final revelation, but the present period of experience, as the preceding sentence and the following verse make most natural. **Shall assure** (or, *persuade*). Co-ordinate with 'shall know,' and springing out of the same condition of love. **Our hearts.** As the seat of moral feeling, conscience, yielding disturbing accusation or pacifying approval. The tenor of the next verse makes this evident. The term elsewhere may include other springs of feeling. 'To persuade our hearts' is to make a plea before them as if they were judges; to satisfy the questionings of conscience, to bring it upon our side, so that it clears us and speaks peace. Of course, guilt and fear are removed from the conscience by the blood of Christ, but the full assurance of this work in its peaceful effects comes in connection with brotherly love, not apart from it. If the love be absent, the assurance of forgiveness, the consciousness of a clean conscience, are absent also. Love does not cleanse the conscience, but it supplies to it a satisfying argument that the guilt is taken away. One grace may be the advocate and light of another.

20. For if our heart condemn (know aught against) **us** (it is because), **God is greater than our heart and knoweth all things.** Hence, if conscience is assured, it must be before God. John gives this verse as the reason (ὅτι) for emphasizing 'before him' (ἔμπροσθεν αὐτοῦ) in connection with the assuring of the heart, in the preceding sentence. 'Before him' has the place of emphasis, and upon it hinges our present verse. This is so evident that the wonder is how the expositors could generally miss this key of the interpretation, as they have done. If conscience is persuaded and pacified merely in and by itself, that may be insufficient; but if it be done under the searching eye and full knowledge of God, then it is well done; and not otherwise can it be well done, since God is greater than our conscience and knows all things, and his holiness and knowledge must judge more perfectly. Conscience, "if not forcibly stopped, naturally and always goes on to anticipate a *higher* and more effectual sentence, which shall hereafter second and affirm its own." (Bishop Butler.) In the presence of brotherly love, the heart is peaceful in its own court and in God's. The second 'because' states the reason for the heart's condemnation. That condemnation is the echo of the voice of him who is greater and knows all things. The reason of the heart's sentence is back in God himself. In the action of conscience, therefore, there is a certain revelation of God. The relation of the word 'because' we have indicated in the translation by assuming an ellipsis, and sup-

21 Beloved, if our heart condemn us not, *then* have we confidence toward God.
22 And whatsoever we ask, we receive of him, because we keep his commandments, and do those things that are pleasing in his sight.
23 And this is his commandment, That we should

22 demn us not, we have boldness toward God; and
whatsoever we ask, we receive of him, because we
keep his commandments, and do the things that
23 are pleasing in his sight. And this is his commandment, that we should [1] believe in the name of his

1 *Gr. believe the name.*

plying the simple words 'it is.' The ellipsis is not foreign to John's peculiar style. See 2: 19; 3: 12.

21, 22. Beloved. See note on ver. 2. **If our heart condemn us not.** Being pacified in the presence of God. **Then have we confidence** (or *boldness*) **toward God.** Which is an advance upon a state of peace. This boldness is the sense of freedom and confidence. See note under 2: 28. When free from condemnation, we are more than free; we look up to God in perfect childlike confidence, and so come boldly unto a throne of grace. See next sentence. **And whatsoever we ask** (in the confidence just spoken of) **we receive of** (from, ἀπὸ, not παρά) **him**—namely, from God, to whom we come with freedom of conscience and supplication. The asking is that of those who are in the sphere of brotherly love, and bear the name of beloved. It is one form which the spiritual freedom of the child in his Father's house takes. God receives it as a proof of our confidence in him if we ask him for what we need, and he is not annoyed, but pleased. The free feeling toward God must go out in prayer. And the asking that comes of this child-spirit of the life of divine love, will be in faith, and in the Holy Spirit, and according to the will of God; and whatsoever a Christian asks of God with these conditions, he will receive from him, whether it be a temporal good or a spiritual grace. That word '*whatsoever*' is of wonderful range, and includes temporal things as much as it does spiritual; but it is true of him who prays in union with God and in the Spirit of supplications. (Zech. 12: 10; Rom. 8: 26.) The prayer, then, for small thing or great is a divine thought. Like a river, the spiritual child's prayer flows down into the ocean of God, and returns in dews and rains upon him. True prayer corresponds to the system of veins and arteries in the human body—life rising to the heart and coming from the heart. **Because we keep his commandments.** This marks the thoroughly obedient spirit that underlies effectual praying, and recalls the already implied relation of such praying to loving the brethren. For the commandments spoken of include in particular, as in 2: 3, the one on which John has dwelt so much, that of loving a brother with the love of Christ. The man who does this, which is the very essence of obedience, will obey in other things, and he will pray effectually for all things that truly concern him. (Ps. 138: 8.) He is the righteous man of whom James speaks, and whose fervent prayer availeth much. He is the righteous one to whose cry the ears of Jehovah are open, as the Psalmist declares. As a rule, save in the case of the sinner first crying for pardon, effectual praying is the fruit of a godly tree. "If ye *abide* in me, and my words *abide* in you, ye shall ask what ye will, and it shall be done unto you." (John 15: 7.) It is not the occasional exertion of a lean, disobedient soul; it is the overflow of an habitual spirituality. **And do those things that are pleasing in his sight.** Keeping the commandments, especially that enjoining brotherly love, is beautiful in his sight, and is a reflection of his own nature. We ought to keep the commandments, in order to please God.

23. And connects the previous reference to commandments with an added unfolding definition. **This is his commandment**—namely, a brotherly love with its root in belief in Christ, or belief in Christ with its outgrowth in brotherly love; for so are they viewed as one by the writer, and called one commandment. They are inseparable. Inevitably, faith works by love. But though they develop as vitally one, they have a logical order, which is given in the statement of the verse. John's word surely suggests that what is cardinal in Christianity is belief in the Lord Jesus, and brotherly love, developed in a gracious unity. The term 'his' has its natural antecedent in God. **That** (ἵνα) states the end as well as substance of God's command. The command looks directly to the act of obedience, as well as the rule of it.

believe on the name of his Son Jesus Christ, and love one another, as he gave us commandment.

24 And he that keepeth his commandments dwelleth in him, and he in him. And hereby we know that he abideth in us, by the Spirit which he hath given us.

Son Jesus Christ, and love one another, even as he
24 gave us commandment. And he that keepeth his
commandments abideth in him, and he in him.
And hereby we know that he abideth in us, by the
Spirit that he gave us.

CHAPTER IV.

BELOVED, believe not every spirit, but try the spirits whether they are of God: because many false prophets are gone out into the world.

1 Beloved, believe not every spirit, but prove the

Believing on the name (dative because that to which the action is given and on which it terminates) of Jesus Christ is believing in him as fulfilling all that his name and his revelation express. "It is to believe the gospel message concerning him, and him as living in it in all his fullness." (Alford.) **As he** (Christ) **gave us commandment.** If 'he' were God, the present statement would only repeat practically the first words of the verse. But making it Christ, the writer adds the confirmation and pattern of a well-known historical fact.

24. And resumes the subject of keeping the commandments (plural) begun in the last part of ver. 22. **He that keepeth his commandments.** Including the double cardinal command of ver. 23, and others. In the present verse these commands are referred to Christ as their author, to whom the last preceding words have called the writer's thought. The following words about a mutual indwelling refer more naturally to Christ, and to some of his very words in the Gospel of John. The ease with which our apostle can glide, in thought and affirmation, from Father to Son, in the discussions of truth and grace, shows what equal honor and what relation of unity they had in his mind. On the keeping of the commands, see note under 2: 3. The abiding of us in union with Christ, and of him in union with us, is presented as something which attends, accompanies, goes along with, keeping his commands, and is evidenced by this keeping, and is itself in turn fostered by it. **And hereby**—namely, by the Spirit given us. **We know.** As a continuous consciousness. **That he** (Christ) **abideth in us.** This is a matter of realization, of a knowledge as certain to us as a part of ourselves. From what shall such assurance spring? **By the Spirit which he** (Christ) **hath given** (or *gave*) **us.** 'Us' Christians, when we believed. The gift of the Holy Spirit is from the Father. But it is also from the Son, as many passages show. The Spirit, dwelling in us as a personal presence, reveals and witnesses of our union with Christ. It is his office to make our new life a consciousness. And this gift of the Spirit, working this knowledge, is the privilege of all believers. But not all who profess to have the Spirit have received him; hence the need of caution, which leads on to the earnest charge in the following section.

Ch. 4: 1-6. THE DUTY AND METHOD OF TESTING THOSE WHO COME TO US CLAIMING TO HAVE THE HOLY SPIRIT.

This is the occasion of bringing to view once more (see 2: 18) the false teachers, or antichrists. The apostle severely exposes them, and utters a sharp warning against them. We discover some reason why John should be called Boanerges.

1. Beloved. Set off against the enemies and errorists. See explanation under 3: 2. All who appreciate the new nature love them. Possibly we are too reserved in applying this name. **Believe not every spirit.** Here John refers to the spirits of men, considered as having religious capacity, and under the influence of the Spirit of God or the spirit of antichrist. At the close of the preceding chapter one might say: "But shall I take the word of every man who says he has the Spirit? Is a man's saying he has the Spirit enough for me? May I receive him on this?" "No," says John, "it is your bounden duty, and I command you not to believe every spirit, but to test every one thoroughly. Use reasonable tests to find out whether the spirit of him who comes to you with his religious claims has been truly imbued with God's Spirit, or is under some other influence." The command suggests that we should carefully examine and prove all who apply for a place in Christ's Church, as well as those who assume to be Christian teachers. By implication it forbids building up the Church with an

2 **Hereby know ye the Spirit of God: Every spirit that confesseth that Jesus Christ is come in the flesh is of God:**

3 **And every spirit that confesseth not that Jesus Christ is come in the flesh is not of God: and this is**

spirits, whether they are of God; because many
2 **false prophets are gone out into the world. Here-**
by know ye the Spirit of God: every spirit that
confesseth that Jesus Christ is come in the flesh is
3 **of God: and every spirit that [1] confesseth not Jesus**
is not of God: and this is the *spirit* of the anti-

[1] Some ancient authorities read *annulleth Jesus.*

unconverted membership or recognizing an unregenerate ministry. We may mistake, but we are bound to use all reasonable means to discriminate. **Of God.** Allied to him in spiritual nature. **Because.** Reason making the trial necessary and urgent. One might ask: "Have any claimed to have the Holy Spirit, who are false in that claim?" "Yes," says the apostle; "and not a few, but many." The many false prophets are the same as the many antichrists of 2: 18. A prophet is one who speaks for another. The false prophet professes to speak for God and under his inspiration, as the antichrist falsely claims to be on the side of Christ and to represent his teaching. **Are gone out.** From the ranks of Christian profession (2: 19), and are now abroad spreading their errors in the world.

2. Hereby—or, in the operation of the test about to be stated. **Know ye** (or, *ye know*). The moment the test is named. With Alford, against almost all, we prefer the indicative to the imperative. It is more in John's confidential manner, and sounds more like the occasional *in this we know.* **The Spirit of God.** The Holy Spirit (of 3: 24) identifying himself with the human spirit to which he is given; the Holy Spirit working in men's spirits. This is the common view; probably the better view. Yet the spirit, whichever one it is, that belongs to God, may be meant. **Every spirit that confesseth.** Not merely once, but right on. The confession is something uttered before men. Unexpressed confession is a contradiction of terms, and a thing impossible. As Lange suggests, the very word means the oral confession of a truth or reality. Such confession is one of the fixed laws of the new life. There is no heavenly promise for him who is unwilling to confess Christ before men. The Bible does not own such an one as having salvation. (Rom. 10: 9, 10.) **That Jesus Christ is come in the flesh.** The matter of the confession is not the mere name of Christ, which even the errorists confessed; but it is Christ in his genuine nature and office, having a particular history, and embodying a particular system of truth. It is that he is Jesus, and therefore the Saviour of a people. It is that he is Christ, and therefore the Anointed of God. It is that this Christ Jesus has come from God in the flesh, in a real, not a seeming humanity, with the soul and body of human nature. When John wrote, men were beginning to teach that Christ only appeared to have a human nature, as the angels who came to Lot and Manoah; and, being astray on the incarnation of Christ, they were necessarily at fault as to his priestly work and his saving power. It was but the divergence of a step, some might say, but it really involved a denial of the gospel salvation by the God-man, Christ, and his real death; and a person could not deny that essential scheme of salvation and be saved by it at the same time. This is a fearful warning to such as are not docile enough to receive the nature and work of Christ as they are; who wish to explain this or that away, who diverge by a little, as it seems from the total faith. In particular, we must believe aright concerning Christ. Gospel truth is of a definite type, which the regenerate will not miss. The spiritual mind will take to it as naturally as the bird to the air or the bee to its clover. It does make a difference what a man believes. **Is of God.** Is allied to him in spiritual nature through regeneration.

3. That confesseth not Jesus. '*The* Jesus' (τὸν Ἰησοῦν) that is set forth, and as he is set forth, in the foregoing verse; and hence omitting the words, **Christ is come in the flesh,** here given by the Common Version, but rejected by the critical text. The subjective negative (μὴ) before the word 'confesseth' suggests a wilful refusal. The Douay Version (Roman Catholic) renders this part of the verse, "that dissolveth Jesus" (!), without the support of any present manuscript. Suppose the one refusing to confess Jesus and his true office and nature, should be sincere, that does not alter the cardinal fact of his standing; he is not of (ἐκ) God. **And** (moreover) **this** (spirit not confessing

that *spirit* of antichrist, whereof ye have heard that it should come; and even now already is it in the world.
4 Ye are of God, little children, and have overcome them: because greater is he that is in you, than he that is in the world.
5 They are of the world: therefore speak they of the world, and the world heareth them.
6 We are of God: he that knoweth God heareth us;

christ, whereof ye have heard that it cometh; and
4 now it is in the world already. Ye are of God, *my*
little children, and have overcome them: because greater is he that is in you than he that is
5 in the world. They are of the world: therefore
speak they *as* of the world, and the world heareth
6 them. We are of God: he that knoweth God heareth us; he who is not of God heareth us not. By

Christ in his true nature) **is that spirit of antichrist** (literally, *the antichrist*) **whereof ye have heard that it should come** (literally, *cometh*). This is the spirit answering to, and identified with, the spirit of antichrist. The Christian professor who has this spirit is an antichrist. See full explanation of the word 'cometh,' and especially of 'antichrist,' under 2: 18. Let it be recalled and emphasized, that an antichrist is not one who denies Christ outright; but one who, claiming to receive him, attributes to him such a nature, work, or doctrine as really makes another Christ of him. The name may be given to one so doing, or to the common spirit pervading all who do this. Along all the gospel age, this "man of sin" (2 Thess. 2: 3) has his types, men who, claiming the Christian name, are perverting the fundamental doctrine it represents.

4. Ye (emphatic) **are of God, little children, and have overcome them.** 'Little children' (note on 2: 1) were they; not boastful, not overbearing, not conceited, not originators of a religious philosophy of their own, not in haste to say what God ought to do and Christ ought to be; but men and women of the child-spirit, willing to receive Christ as he is, his word as he gave it, willing to confess the Lord Jesus in all his nature, work, truth; trusting, docile, obedient; such they were, and as such were of God, born of him, belonging to him, having his Spirit; tried by the tests, and not found wanting. And they had 'overcome' (Johannean word) those who had made other confession and were of a different spirit. They were not caught with their delusions, nor led into their snares. In all their contests with them they had triumphed, and should triumph. The shout of a king was among them. The errorists might be more eloquent, higher up in the social scale, more learned, but the little ones having the truth were the conquering people. **Because greater is he that is in you than he that is in the world.** The reason of the prevalence of spiritual men is not in themselves. They need not take personal credit. The one in them, in union with their hearts, is God; naturally suggested by the previous clause, and by the relation of terms in 3: 10. The one 'in the world,' in union with the men of the world, is the devil. (John 11: 30; 2 Cor. 4: 4; Eph. 2: 2.) The world is a more general term than antichrist. All outside of God's light and life are of the world; while antichrist includes those who profess Christ but make him another Christ. But the latter belong also to the wider class of the world, as John's reasoning assumes; and if so, he that is in the world is in them. And God is stronger than he. Which the overcoming side is, therefore, cannot be doubtful.

5. They are of (ἐκ) **the world.** Of one nature with it. What the preceding words had implied as to the belonging of the false teachers is now expressly stated. They may be enrolled in some church bearing the Christian name; they may profess to be the only consistent expounders of Christianity; they may claim the Spirit divine; but in truth they are of the world, wholly under worldly motives, still unconverted, still in their sins. They may have a strong religiousness, but not the Spirit of God. **Therefore speak they of** (ἐκ) **the world.** Their doctrine necessarily partakes of the worldly nature within them and about them. They teach a system congenial to worldly men. **And the world heareth them.** "Adopts readily their teaching so accordant with its own spirit." (Hackett.) The world loves its own. See John 8: 47; 15: 19; 17: 14. How much in the circle of his Master's teaching and very words is John. Wonderful receptivity!

6. We (emphatic) **are of** (ἐκ) **God.** Allied to him in spiritual nature through the new birth; in contrast with the antichrists. And so in sympathy with God's doctrine, and speaking it. By 'we' John means especially himself and the true teachers, not excluding, however, any of the spiritual party. The Church speaks doctrine through its teachers. **He that knoweth God heareth us. Ex-**

he that is not of God heareth not us. Hereby know we the spirit of truth, and the spirit of error.
7 Beloved, let us love one another: for love is of God; and every one that loveth is born of God, and knoweth God.

this we know the spirit of truth, and the spirit of error.
7 Beloved, let us love one another: for love is of God; and every one that loveth is begotten of God,

perimental knowledge, knowledge that receives its object. The hearing is more than that of the ear; it is willing adoption of the teaching, as being consonant with the heart's knowledge of God. The heart and the doctrine are in one sphere. **He that is not of God, heareth not us.** For the reason just suggested. It is not the spiritual mind (John 10: 8), but the unspiritual, that goes after the errorists, that prefers human philosophy to the true word. **Hereby know we.** That is, from the criteria just mentioned. What one most readily hears, shows what spirit he is of, to what nature or sphere he belongs. The knowledge is that of quality, hence the knowledge of discrimination. **The Spirit of truth, and the spirit of error.** As they are in men. The Spirit of truth is the Holy Spirit (John 14: 17) in his relation to truth. The spirit of error is the devil in his fontal relation to all false doctrine. He who welcomes Christ's doctrines has the Spirit who gives them. He whose soul takes naturally to false doctrine is in affinity with the arch seducer, liar, and wanderer. The closing words of the section look back to the opening words.

7-13. CHRISTIAN LOVE ENJOINED IN NEW CONNECTIONS. IT IS THE EVIDENCE THAT WE ARE BORN OF GOD, THAT WE KNOW GOD, THAT WE APPRECIATE GOD'S LOVE TO US, AND THAT GOD IS DWELLING IN US.

John resumes the great theme of brotherly love with which he closed the last chapter; "but this time in nearer and deeper connection with our birth from God, and knowledge of him who is himself love." (Alford.) Having just spoken of signs of the presence of the Spirit; he is led again to that great demonstration of the new life afforded in the exercise of love. Love, he maintains is not only a duty, but belongs to the very nature of our divine kinship through regeneration; and hence, if wanting, our divine life is without reality.

7. Beloved. See notes on 3: 2; 4: 1. **Let us love one another.** See note on 3: 18. How much John dwells on this grace! How large a part of Christianity it is to him! Along with faith, with which it is organically one, it is paramount. (3: 23.) Faith unites to Christ; and love, to each other. New convictions of the importance and indispensableness of brotherly love come with the study of this Epistle. More plainly we see that he who has it not is not a Christian, however correct he may be in other respects. A new heart will not be persistently hard toward a brother. That is a fixed point. To carry hatred and spite into the fellowship of Christ's Church, is to carry in the spirit of Cain and the devil. It is to take a piece of hell into heaven. What this love is, as distinguished from general benevolence and neighborliness, has been fully stated. It is the family affection of God's house, as peculiar, as exclusive, as a mother's love for her own child. Did not Jesus love John otherwise than he did Herod and Caiaphas? This love of spiritual kinship, like the gift of the Spirit, distinguishes Christianity generically from all other religions. It takes it from their category. Let it be added that it is a grace which we are called to exercise, not toward perfect or agreeable Christians only, but toward very imperfect and not wholly congenial Christians; for many such there are. We must exercise a love that, going through the imperfections of a brother, loves him for Christ's sake, even at the cost of self-denial. If Christ loved us, as some Christians bestow their love—namely, on a principle of loving only agreeable Christians, where might we stand? **For love is of God.** Of one nature with him. Not natural love, which all men have, but Christian love. It is not anything we have by nature; does not spring out of natural relationships; is not born of the flesh; does not belong to the plane of earthly loves; is not, as some have said, natural love directed to new objects; but is a heavenly principle, created in us out of the very nature of God; in God before it was in us. (Rom. 5: 5.) "The appetite for good is from God, the unchangeable good; which appetite is love, of which John saith, 'Love is of God.' Not that its beginning is of us, and its perfecting of God, but that the whole of love is from God." (Augustine.) **And every one that loveth**

8 He that loveth not, knoweth not God; for God is love.
9 In this was manifested the love of God toward us, because that God sent his only begotten Son into the world, that we might live through him.

8 and knoweth God. He that loveth not knoweth
9 not God; for God is love. Herein was the love of
God manifested [1]in us, that God hath sent his only
begotten Son into the world, that we might live
10 through him. Herein is love, not that we loved

[1] Or, *in our case.*

is born (or, *begotten*) **of God and knoweth God.** Love is the evidence of the new birth and of spiritual knowledge. If one has this divine principle, it proves that he himself has a nature from God and an experience of God. Love is the predicate of the renewed state, and the logical development of spiritual knowledge.

8. He that loveth not, knoweth (or, *knew*) **not God.** That is, never knew God at any time; or perhaps when he professed such knowledge. The past tense makes the statement peculiarly significant and strong. **For God is love.** The expression is one of the deepest in the Bible. Its meaning will ever grow in the mind of the growing Christian, and still be unfathomable. It is said not alone of the loving action of God, not alone of the tender feelings of God, but of the very nature of God. Love is a component of his being, the conscious state of his being. There is no part of his nature that is wanting in this element. It is co-extensive with his life. One, therefore, who in the new birth gets something of God's nature, must get a portion of the divine love. It is simply impossible to be born from above, without receiving this principle. He, therefore, who does not love, in the Christian sense, is not spiritually related to him, and hence does not know him, and cannot. Or, he that loves not, knows not love; and if he knows not love, he knows not God, for God is love. A close texture of truth. [Compare the statements, "God is a spirit," John 4: 24; "God is light," 1 John 1: 5, with this "God is love."—A. H.]

9. In this—namely, in sending the Divine Son with the motive of our salvation. **Was manifested the love of God toward us.** [Rather, *in us*—ἐν ἡμῖν.—A. H.] That is, at the time of our conversion, by means of the salvation-facts we then became experimentally acquainted with. Thus were manifested the fact, nature, and degree of the love of God. **Because that** (better, as in Revised Version, *that*, the fact that; declarative, not causal) **God sent** (*hath sent*); sent from himself in heaven, involving the personal pre-existence of the One sent. Hath sent forth at a particular moment in the past; but the event is viewed as prolonged in its operation, and in its vital relation to the experience of believers; hence the perfect tense. **His only begotten Son** "expresses an unique kindredship of nature, and involves a correspondent affection (Ps. 22: 20, Septuagint) of him who begat; expresses an eternal relation, not eternal generation." (Hackett.) The term 'only begotten' (μονογενής) is applied to the only child of earthly parents in three instances by Luke (7: 12; 8: 42; 9: 38), and once in Heb. 11: 17. Otherwise it is used in the New Testament only by John, and by him applied to the Son of God. The total expression seems, in our passage at least, to mark a relation of a filial nature held by the Son before he came in the flesh, and making it especially the proof of divine love that he should be sent forth. At the same time, it must be said, that the event of the incarnation is sufficient of itself to justify the full title, or either part of it. All true Christians are, in an important sense, sons of God, having been "begotten again unto a lively hope" (1 Peter 1: 3), and having "received the spirit of adoption, whereby we cry, Abba, Father." (Rom. 8: 15.) "As many as are led by the Spirit of God, they are the sons (υἱοὶ) of God." (Rom. 8: 14.) But Christ is not merely *a* Son of God, he is *the* Son, having the full nature of God, bearing a unique relation to him in eternity itself, as well as having a unique history in the incarnation. For the Father to give up such a Son for a mission into this world of rebellion and sin was no ordinary test or manifestation of love. Some picture of it would be to send our dearest one into a lazaretto to save the dying, or into a camp of rebels to proffer conditions of peace. **That we might live through him.** The intention of Christ's mission. An effectual, and not a contingent, purpose, as regards believers. The object of the mission, having reference to our greatest good, impresses us with God's love, as does

10 Herein is love, not that we loved God, but that he loved us, and sent his Son *to be* the propitiation for our sins.
11 Beloved, if God so loved us, we ought also to love one another.
12 No man hath seen God at any time. If we love one another, God dwelleth in us, and his love is perfected in us.
13 Hereby know we that we dwell in him, and he in us, because he hath given us of his Spirit

God, but that he loved us, and sent his Son *to be* the
11 propitiation for our sins. Beloved, if God so loved
12 us, we also ought to love one another. No man
hath beheld God at any time: if we love one
another, God abideth in us, and his love is perfect-
13 ed in us: hereby know we that we abide in him,
and he in us, because he hath given us of his Spirit.

the self-sacrificing means to effect it. The giving up of the Son, the giving him to come into such a world, and the thoughtful, merciful object of the mission, combine to give the believer an impressive view of the extent and the quality of God's love. The 'living' is the true immortality reached in regeneration and resurrection through the mediation (διά) of Christ. The whole verse condenses a volume of truth. It is a remarkable statement of the mission of Christ, and its spring in the eternal love of God. It demonstrates the love-nature asserted in the foregoing verse.

10. Herein is love. In its full nature, so as to be marked and known. This love is not manifested by the fact that we Christians have loved God. That is not extraordinary. But it is by the fact that he loved us back in eternity, without any love in us as the motive; and in the additional fact that, self-moved, he sent his own Son a propitiation in respect to our sins. Compare Rom. 5: 8. Loving sinners, so as to redeem them by the work of the atonement, is love. There you see it, and see what it is. On this work of propitiation, see note on 2: 1, 2. Through our present passage, the soul of John Milne, as a convicted sinner, was brought into light and peace.

11. Beloved. See on 3: 2; 4: 1. The term introduces a fervent appeal and faithful admonition. The influence of such a word under such circumstances is obvious. **If God so** (emphatic) **loved us** (while we were yet sinners, and so much as to sacrifice his Son for us) **we ought also** (better, *we also ought*) **to love one another.** We ought surely to love our own brethren, if he loved us sinners; and to love them enough to sacrifice something for them. It is the argument from the greater to the less. The argument of gratitude is implied. Also the argument of the new nature; since where is our likeness to God if we do not love, as he is proved to have done?

12. No man hath seen (*beheld*) **God at any time.** Although this opening is apparently abrupt, yet the connection of thought between this verse and the preceding is evident and simple: We ought to love one another; and, though we may not see God with these outward eyes, yet if we thus love, God is in us as really as if we saw him. He is where his love is, for love, as a divine principle, is a part of himself. God the Father is the one spoken of, and that beholding of him, which has thus far been denied to mortal man, is of the bodily eyes. Men have seen, with the outward vision, the express image of the Father in Jesus Christ (Heb. 1: 3; John 14: 9), but not God the Father by himself as he is. (John 1: 18.) He whom Adam and Abraham and Moses saw was not the Father, but the Word, the Angel of Jehovah, the veiled higher nature of Christ before he came in the flesh. **If we love one another, God dwelleth** (or, *abideth*) **in us.** God is where his love is, for it is inseparable from himself. It is himself, just as his Spirit is. Love is of God in nature and source. (Ver. 7.) Loving one another, in the spiritual sense, is the exercise of God's nature in us. The loving heart contains him; Jehovah-Shammah. **And his love** (the one divine principle of love whether in him or in us) **is perfected in us.** Made complete, brought to maturity. This happens when, experiencing God's love in us, we love one another. A tree reaches maturity, fulfills its end, in bearing fruit. The same is true of the plant of divine love in the heart. Brotherly love is God's love fulfilling its end and bearing fruit.

13. Hereby (or, *in this*)—namely, in the fact that God has given us the Holy Spirit—**we know that we dwell** (or, *abide*) **in him, and he in us.** See 3: 24, where the same words are used of our union with Christ, following John 15: 4, 5. Here the apostle means our union with God the Father, so easy is the transition in thought or experience from Son to Father,

14 And we have seen and do testify that the Father
sent the Son *to be* the Saviour of the world.
15 Whosoever shall confess that Jesus is the Son of
God, God dwelleth in him, and he in God.
16 And we have known and believed the love that

14 And we have beheld and bear witness that the
Father hath sent the Son *to be* the Saviour of the
15 world. Whosoever shall confess that Jesus is the
Son of God, God abideth in him, and he in God.
16 And we know and have believed the love which

so natural is it to honor the one as the other, so fitted are the divine predicates to the one or the other. If we are united to Christ, we are united to God in Christ. In ver. 12, John had said, if we love, God abides in us; but can this be known? "Yes," says he, "we may know it, we do know it, as true, in the strongest possible statement of it. Our divine union, which our love implies, is a matter of certain knowledge. It is a fact of experience. We know it as much as we know our existence." How do we know it? By what evidence? By this—**Because he hath given us of his Spirit.** For his presence in us declares the fact; and his voice in us is witness to the fact. The Spirit in our hearts is the seal and assurance of our union with God. It is the very element and life of the union. He that is joined to the Lord is one Spirit. The gift of the Spirit carries with it every fact of the new life. It proves all. The root of love in us is God, whose presence the Spirit certifies and reveals.

14-16. THE FACT OF THE MUTUAL INDWELLING OF GOD AND THE CHRISTIAN IS ASSURED TO US IN THE VERY TERMS OF SALVATION; AND IN OUR KNOWLEDGE OF THE LOVE OF GOD IN US.

This is additional to the assurance of the Spirit. The actual spiritual connection of God with the soul of the renewed man is something which John would strongly declare and confirm. Our divine union is a first truth with him.

14. And takes up a new and additional line of proof of the living union of God and his people. **We.** The Christian party, through the apostles. **Have seen** (or *beheld*). Have the evidence of our own eyes, accompanied with careful contemplation. See 1: 1, 2. **And do testify** (or, *bear witness*). Continue to do so, as witnessing to the gospel facts is not for once. **That the Father.** So named here from his relation to Christ, rather than to John. **Sent** (better, *hath sent*). In the past, but the influence and effects are still present. See on ver. 9. **The Son to be the** (better, *a*) **Saviour of the world.** 'Saviour' is a distinctive title of the Son, declaring the mission on which he was sent into the world. He was sent to provide, in his own person, salvation for the world, which salvation is availed of and actually applied, through belief and confession. See Rom. 10: 9, and our next verse. See notes in full on 2: 2. To those who receive him, the Son of God is Saviour from what? From guilt and condemnation, from despair, from a nature of sin, from error, from a body of death, from the world, from Satan, from an eternal hell; requiring a great Saviour, with all his deity and all his humanity, all his blood and all his Spirit.

15. Whosoever shall confess. As a part of the plan by which Christ becomes an effectual Saviour. It is a stipulation under the salvation proclaimed in the preceding verse, which explains the mood and tense. The confession is that from the inmost being, from the whole being, uttered openly and with the mouth. [It seems to me that the aorist subjective is here used in the sense of the Latin future-perfect; thus, "Whoever shall have confessed that Jesus is the Son of God," etc. Yet the translation given by the Revised English Bible, the Bible Union, and by Alford, Noyes, and others, namely: "Whoever confesseth," etc., is sufficiently exact. The Latin Vulgate reads: *Quisquis confessus fuerit.* Compare Winer, § 43. 3. b.; Buttmann, "Grammar of the New Testament Greek," p. 219; and "Proceedings of the Am. Phil. Association for 1877," pp. 22, 23.—A. H.] **That Jesus** (the man) **is** (also) **the Son of God.** This is the matter of the saving confession, or the basal part of it. See on ver. 2. **God dwelleth** (or, *abideth*) **in him.** In that man who thus confesses, whosoever he is, and however great a sinner. A simple statement of fact included under the very provision and terms of salvation by Christ, sealed by apostolic testimony. **And he in God.** This completes the expression of the perfect living union of God and the regenerate soul.

16. And introduces an additional confirmation of the living union with God, co-ordinate with that in ver. 14, 15. **We have**

God hath to us. God is love; and he that dwelleth in love dwelleth in God, and God in him.
17 Herein is our love made perfect, that we may have boldness in the day of judgment: because as he is, so are we in this world.
18 There is no fear in love; but perfect love casteth

God hath [1] in us. God is love; and he that abideth in love abideth in God, and God abideth in him.
17 Herein is love made perfect with us, that we may have boldness in the day of judgment; because as he
18 is, even so are we in this world There is no fear in
love: but perfect love casteth out fear, because fear

1 Or, *in our case.*

known and believed. Another certainty additional to the 'we have seen' in ver. 14, and in the same tense. That was the certainty of sight; this of experience. The saying that we have both 'known and believed' suggests the intimate relation of spiritual knowledge and belief. They both have as their object things invisible, and doubtless they are commingled in one act of a soul coming into life. "True faith is a faith of knowledge and experience; true knowledge is a knowledge of faith." (Lücke.) Note the order of the verbs. There is a persuasion that comes of experience. **The love that God hath to (*in*) us.** Not "in regard to us" (Alford), but literally *in us*. In the new life we have experienced a new principle of love in our hearts which we have intuitively recognized as something from God, as his love in us, the love he has in us. Now, John, recalling the proposition in ver. 8, says **God is love,** and hence this love of his in us, which we know and believe, is God himself. And, of course, then, it follows that **he that dwelleth** (or, *abideth*) **in love** (as he does who has God's love in him) **dwelleth** (or, *abideth*) **in God** (emphatic), **and God in him.** In ver. 12, the point is the fact of our union with God, implied in our love. Here the point is the assurance or confirmation of the fact, derived from our personal experience of love.

17-21. Further Comments on Spiritual Love: (1) In Perfection, it takes away Fear; (2) Its Exercise toward God Accounted for; (3) Love to God Implies Love to Our Brother.

17. Herein. In the personal *experience* of love, and especially of the union with God which it implies, just spoken of; expressing the manner or means of love's perfection with us. Or, in this interest, with this intention—namely, that we may have boldness in the day of judgment; expressing the end or purpose of love's perfection with us. Either explanation is worthy; the former possibly having the preference. Other constructions seem improbable. **Is our love made perfect.** The Revised Version is correct: *Is love made perfect with us* (μεθ' ἡμῶν). Love has been perfected, matured, fulfilled, not in itself, but with us, in the conscious life and fruit-bearing of our souls. **That** (ἵνα, *for this end that*) **we may have boldness in the day of** (*the*) **judgment** states a divine end of the perfection of love with us. It is that we may, being full of divine love, and carrying along with us the calm consciousness of being one with God thereby produced, meet the searching judgment of the last day, free from all sense of condemnation and perfect in confidence. In perfected love there is a conscious union with God that makes us bold and confident before the divine Judge himself. See 2: 28; 3: 19-21. In this union we cannot be condemned any more than God himself. Judgment is coming, but he who is hid in the pavilion of God's nature is as safe and confident as was Noah in the ark. **Because as he is, so** (or, *even so*) **are we in this world** expands and states more explicitly the reason, or rather philosophy, of this complete confidence in the judgment day. 'He,' or, *that one*, is he before whom we shall come in that great day, whether it be God, or, as generally understood, Christ, viewed as possessing the divine nature. The reasoning is: This confidence we shall have at the judgment, because, in the love and union of God with us, we shall bear there a nature already one with that of him who will judge us. As he is, in his spiritual nature, in the other world, so by divine union are we already in this world, and that likeness of nature will insure confidence in the day of judgment. This explanation is quite harmonious with that basis of love and divine indwelling on which the apostle is arguing, and seems almost self-evident. Notwithstanding, we have Ebrard saying, "We contemplate the words in question without any clear conception of their meaning!"

18. There is no fear in love. In the great divine principle of love, whether in God or in us. In it there is no fear, no servile fear,

out fear: because fear hath torment. He that feareth is not made perfect in love.
19 We love him, because he first loved us.
20 If a man say, I love God, and hateth his brother, he is a liar: for he that loveth not his brother whom he hath seen, how can he love God whom he hath not seen?

hath punishment; and he that feareth is not made
19 perfect in love. We love, because he first loved
20 us. If a man say, I love God, and hateth his brother, he is a liar: for he that loveth not his brother whom he hath seen, [1]cannot love God whom he
21 hath not seen. And this commandment have we

1 Many ancient authorities read *how can he love God whom he hath not seen?*

no fear of condemnation or punishment, no fear that hath the least pain in it. The love in God cannot have any of this. The love in us, one in nature, cannot have any of it. Yet there is a fear, not now in the apostle's thought, which is consistent with spiritual love, and perhaps a part of it. **But perfect love casteth out fear.** Referring to the presence of divine love in our hearts, and perfected there. In its completeness it fills the soul, and thereby shuts out fear which is in us prior to such love. Two spheres cannot occupy the same place. But how does perfect love in us expel fear? In the experience of it, we feel completely united to God, as it were a part of him. We look out upon the world, upon opposition, upon death, upon judgment itself, from the inclosing being of God, from the canopy, the fortification of his own person. In the consciousness of this union we cannot fear evil, any more than God can fear a part of himself. (Rom. 8: 1.) **Because fear hath torment** (better, *punishment*). For thus we must render this last word (κόλασις). Compare the only three other New Testament passages (Matt. 25: 46; Acts 4: 21; 2 Peter 2: 9) where this word, or its root, occurs. It is the punishment of the great day (ver. 17), with which fear is connected, and which it already takes hold upon as if it were a part of itself. "Fear, by anticipating punishment, has it even now; bears about a foretaste of it and so partakes of it." (Alford.) There can be nothing of this, nothing of painful apprehension in love, and therefore the statement in the previous part of the verse must be true. The last proposition in the verse is added (δὲ) as an inference or complement of the words 'perfect love casteth out fear,' and is slightly adversative.

19. We (in contrast with those who fear and have condemnation) **love him.** In the fullest, absolute sense. The word *him* in the Common Version should be omitted, as it is not found in the critical text. The indicative agrees best with the emphatic 'we.' **Because he** (God, ver. 10) **first loved us.** In eternity; and so sent Christ into the world to save us. (Ver. 9.) His love to us preceded our love. It was the cause or reason of ours, which implies in the apostle's thought that it furnished the model or type of ours. Our love is a thing rising from God's love, and so is naturally like it. But God's love went out to men. Ours therefore, to be full and perfect, must (ver. 12) go out to men, even our brethren.

20. If any man say (at any time, aorist), **I love God, and hateth** [better, *hate.* The present subjective is used in this case because the hatred is a continuous feeling.—A. H.] **his brother.** Hating is antithetical to loving. There are no indifferent or neutral moral conditions. In not loving, there is the condition of hating when occasion comes. **He is a liar.** He not only professes falsely, but denies the very nature of love. Our love is the production (ver. 19) of God's love, of one kind with it. But God's love goes out to *us* of the brotherhood. Therefore ours must embrace the same company. If it does not, it is not true love from God. **For.** To make the falsity of the claim still more evident by adducing a principle often illustrated in common life. **He that loveth not his brother.** It is implied in the question that the brother is of the same nature and family with God (5: 1), and hence, like God, is a true object of spiritual love, whether he be seen or unseen. The question also implicitly recognizes the well-known advantage of immediate sight as a means of kindling love for a lovable object. For example, we may love absent Christians, but how is that love enlivened when the social meeting brings them about us. The sight of the eyes moves the heart. (Acts 17: 16.) If, then, we do not love the brother whom we see, how can we, though one may claim it, love him of related nature, whom we have not seen? Can any one tell? This is additional to the consideration that it is the nature of divine love to love the brethren as well as God; and if one is loved, the other is by

21 And this commandment have we from him, That
he who loveth God love his brother also.

from him, that he who loveth God love his brother
also.

CHAPTER V.

WHOSOEVER believeth that Jesus is the Christ is
born of God: and every one that loveth him
that begat loveth him also that is begotten of him.
2 By this we know that we love the children of God,
when we love God, and keep his commandments.

1 Whosoever believeth that Jesus is the Christ is begotten of God: and whosoever loveth him that begat
2 loveth him also that is begotten of him. Hereby
we know that we love the children of God, when

necessity of nature. [It ought perhaps to be noticed that the text approved by Lachmann, Tischendorf, Tregelles, Westcott and Hort has, in the clause before the last, "not" (οὐ) instead of 'how' (πῶς); and we should therefore read, "For he that loveth not his brother cannot love God." The manuscript authority for the common text appears to be inferior to that for the text approved by these editors.—A. H.]

21. And (besides all the rest) **this commandment** (named in the closing part of the verse) **have we from him.** That is, from God; it may be through Christ, and remembered by John as coming from his Master's lips. It is not the commandment embraced in the summary of the law (Matt. 22: 37-39), as claimed by Alford, for that relates to our neighbor, our fellow men in general; while, as we have shown again, the love-command of Christ relates to the inner circle of regenerate men, our brethren in Christ. **That** (ἵνα) introduces not only the purport of the commandment, but the end intended to be secured by it. What an enforcement of love to the brethren! The one loving God must love his brother from gratitude (4: 11), from the divine pattern and nature of love itself (4: 19), from a principle of common sense (4: 20), and now (ver. 20) from the strong command which expresses directly God's will in the matter.

Ch. 5: 1–5. Faith in Jesus as the Christ, the New Birth, Brotherly Love, Keeping Gospel Commands, and Overcoming the World, all Vitally Connected, and Involved in each other.

These principles, obediences, victories, belong to one life, as much so as the branches of one family, root and stalk, flower and fruit. The divine anatomy, the heavenly philosophy, of the new life, is still pursued. There is sweetness, as well as depth, in the subject. It makes the mind work; it also makes the heart warm and glow. Here is the kind of study that will make heaven the happier. Here reasoning and knowledge are also spiritual repast. Blessed are they whose hearts kindle with such themes.

1. Whosoever believeth (from the heart, from the centre of being, with a faith that is a part of one's self) **that Jesus is the Christ** (the one prophesied, and anointed of God) **is born** (or *begotten*) **of God.** From, or out of (ἐκ), God's nature, by the Holy Spirit, and so has become a child in the family. The apostle is setting forth the object to be loved, in the light of its true nature. **And every one that loveth him that begat** (that is God), **loveth him also that is begotten of him**—that is, God's child, of one nature with him. The apostle lays it down as a fact, if we do love God, we also love all that is of his nature, hence we love our brethren who have his nature. It is an argument implied in 4: 20, but here put in unmistakable words, that we may certainly know who the brother to be loved is, and the divine reason of the love to him. Note how much is believed when one believes that Jesus is the Anointed of God, by tracing out the deep truths and facts involved in that wonderful epithet as applied to him. Note also the importance of this verse as a proof-text, bearing upon the relation of regeneration to faith. Shining is the action of the sun; believing is the action of the regenerate heart. Where, then, you see the action of belief, know that regeneration is already, its source.

2. By (or *in*) **this**—namely, in loving God and doing his commands. **We know that we love the children of God.** Those begotten by him, the same spoken of in the preceding verse. How may we know that we love those who have partaken of the divine nature. We may have a kind of love for Christians from various motives, as that they are of our church, sect, or party; are our friends, or are naturally amiable; but we must love them also, and chiefly, because they are the children of God and reflect his

3 For this is the love of God, that we keep his commandments: and his commandments are not grievous.
4 For whatsoever is born of God overcometh the world: and this is the victory that overcometh the world, *even* our faith.

3 we love God, and do his commandments. For this
is the love of God, that we keep his commandments: and his commandments are not grievous.
4 For whatsoever is begotten of God overcometh the
world: and this is the victory that hath overcome the

nature, and for this reason we must love all Christians, and not a select part. But how shall we know if we have this love to God's children as such? **When** (in whatever instance) **we love God,** who is of one spiritual nature with his children, then we may know that our love is spiritual and exercised for spiritual reasons. In 4: 20 love to the brethren proves our love to God. Here the converse proposition emerges. The final reason of loving God's people is in God himself, on a principle that leads us to love them all. **And keep** (literally, *do*, ποιῶμεν, not τηρῶμεν) **his commandments.** Gospel commands; obeyed because they are God's commands, They include belief, confession, baptism, observing the Supper, meeting together, giving, enduring, and the like. He who does these truly, does them from a principle of obedience; has a heart to obey. This man may know that he loves the brethren. For he can discover that his love to the brethren, which is a duty and an obedience, belongs to a general principle of obedience in his heart. Regard for one command is regard for the many. The apostle here, as elsewhere, emphasizes the principle of obedience in the new life. Our love is not all sentiment, but has the strong vigor of duty and obedience. The Christian is an obeying person Or, the connection between doing the commands and loving the brethren may be as follows: He who loves the brethren, loves God; and if he loves God, he regards his will or commands, and does them. So that the doing of the commands becomes an evidence of loving the brethren. This may indicate more truly John's process of thought.

3. For (γάρ) explains the putting together of the two preceding things; loving God and commandment-keeping. **This is the love of God.** This is its nature; its natural working. **That we keep his commandments.** To love another, and be indifferent to his will, is an impossibility, in divine or human relations. So vital is the connection, that it may be said, that to love is to obey. Love prompts obedience, as the life of the vine takes the form of fruit. Let those who profess the love of God, and yet are careless of his commands, be admonished. They are denying the very instinct of the love-nature. The conjunction 'that' (ἵνα), with its verb, anticipates a usage of the modern Greek, and is in place of the infinitive. See Godet, "Com. on John," 1: 27. **And his commandments are not grievous.** 'Are not grievous,' heavy, difficult, to those within the sphere of spiritual life and divine love, as the causal bearing of the next verse implies. See Matt. 11: 30; Gen. 29: 20. Love makes easy and blessed those commands which are crossing to the old nature. In the doing of them difficulties melt away, and there is a sense of freedom and delight. The love that prompts to the command, makes the soul work easily through it. (Ps. 119: 32, 45.) The new nature is, as it were, its own spring and help in all that is required of it, and divine commands are fitted to it, as opportunity is fitted to man.

4. For introduces a reason why the commands are not grievous; it is because in the new birth we come into a state of victory, actually begun, and ideally complete. It is assumed that any difficulty of obedience is caused by the world—that is, by worldly feeling within, or worldly opposition without. The lust of the world and the pride of life in us impart a burdensome aspect to the divine commands; and the world sometimes opposes from without, by tempting, persecution, or otherwise. It is a foe to spiritual obedience. But whatsoever is born of God, overcomes the world; goes on to do so. It has a conquering principle in it, and hence must sweep difficulties out of the way. The conflict will be great sometimes, and the world is not subdued at once; nevertheless, the new nature goes on to victory, and overcomes wholly in the end. For it is like God. **Whatsoever is born** (or, *has been begotten*) **of God.** Whatever; whether it be man, or man's nature, or anything else. "The neuter affirms the universality of the idea more strongly than the masculine." (Hackett.) Compare John 3: 6; 6: 37, 39; 17: 2. **The world.** "Whatever is adverse to God's Spirit. So the de-

5 Who is he that overcometh the world, but he that
believeth that Jesus is the Son of God?
6 This is he that came by water and blood, *even* Jesus
Christ; not by water only, but by water and blood.

5 world, *even* our faith. And who is he that overcometh the world, but he that believeth that Jesus
6 is the Son of God? This is he that came by water
and blood, *even* Jesus Christ: not [1] with the water

1 Gr. *in*.

pravity of our nature is a part of the world." (Calvin.) **And this is the victory that overcometh** (or, *overcame*). The indefinite past (aorist) tense is used. The victory that has overcome in each instance is meant. In every such instance, the victory is looked upon as accomplished, already finished, with the exertion of faith; hence the past tense. **Our faith.** "The identifying of the victory with the faith which gained it is a concise and emphatic way of linking the two inseparably together, so that wherever there is faith there is victory." (Alford.) Faith is the action or means by which the new nature overcomes. And why? Because it appropriates Christ the Conquering One, and identifies us with him. We thus enter into his strength, which is the secret of victory. (John 15: 5; Phil. 4: 13; 1 John 4: 4; also Rom. 7: 24, 25; 1 Cor. 15: 57.) It is, then, faith taking Christ's strength that conquers the world, and every difficulty. Once when McCheyne was feeling almost overcome by the world and sin, these words of John came to him. His faith realized a conquering Christ. He was conscious of relief and victory, and exclaimed, "A wonderful passage!"

5. This verse defines the overcoming faith more expressly, and declares victory impossible without it. As to the faith, it must (1) centre in the personal Christ, (2) take him for what he is, Son of God and Son of man in one true abiding person. Then does he unite himself with the soul, and become its life and its victory. The new nature, then, does not overcome by inaction, but by acting through a definite faith. In the action, the Spirit is received and the power given. But our verse also declares that the world can be overcome in no *other* way. John challenges his readers to produce a single instance of such victory except by this faith in Christ. "Who is the man," he says, "where is he, who ever saw him, that conquers the world but by this gospel faith"? The man does not exist. There is no other principle or means of victory. One might as well think of rising from earth against gravitation, as to think of putting the world under his feet, save by faith in Christ. Without it, the man is a part of the very world he would overcome. But with it, he is united to another sphere, and is lifted above his old self, where he can meet the world at an advantage. Two grave lessons in reform present themselves: (1) One may break off an evil habit, or association, and yet, without gospel faith, have the world reign supreme in him. (2) Mere resolutions, or self-respect, or human religion, or asceticism, or monastic seclusion, will not subdue the world.

6-12. The Witness Without and Within that Jesus is the Son of God and the Container of Life.

The overcoming faith of the former section leads the apostle here to confirm to his readers the object of this faith in his true historical personality as being the source of the eternal life which faith receives.

6. **This is he that came** (in his earthly manifestation) **by** (διά, *through*) **water and blood, even Jesus Christ.** Both true man and the anointed, prophesied, one of God. This is he, this is the very one, who came through (by way of) water and blood, and is witnessed to, in his true life-power, thereby. There has been boundless dispute as to what is meant by the water and the blood, which, connected with our Lord's earthly history, were witnesses of him as the Messiah and the Life. As to the water, some have understood it to be the water that came from the Saviour's pierced side, noted in John 19: 34; some, the baptism enjoined on believers in the Great Commission; some, the word of God. (interpreting the term in John 3: 5 of the same!); some, his own baptism in Jordan. And there are other explanations that need not be mentioned. A careful weighing of the entire section and its purpose leaves hardly a doubt that 'water' refers to our Lord's baptism, a most important event of his earthly manifestation, and pointing, as John 1: 31, 33 shows, to Jesus as the Possessor and Giver of life, and hence the Christ. John calls it by the name of 'water,' because it is the element, rather than the act, of baptism, which

And it is the Spirit that beareth witness, because the Spirit is truth.

7 For there are three that bear record in heaven, the Father, the Word, and the Holy Ghost: and these three are one.

8 And there are three that bear witness in earth, the spirit, and the water, and the blood: and these three agree in one.

9 If we receive the witness of men, the witness of

only, but [1] with the water and [1] with the blood.
7 And it is the Spirit that beareth witness, because the
8 Spirit is the truth. For there are three who bear
witness, the Spirit, and the water, and the blood:
9 and the three agree in one. If we receive the witness of men, the witness of God is greater: for the

[1] Gr. in.

is thought of as the witness. The 'water' of his baptism symbolized the life which he had without measure, or the Spirit of life belonging to him, and hence was a witness that he was truly the Son of God. Is not this the very point John is aiming to establish on various testimonies, that Christ is the Fountain of life? See ver. 11. And if Fountain of life, he is Son of God. And 'blood' is another witness. By the 'blood,' not the Lord's Supper (that is far-fetched, without parallel, and hardly pertinent to the particular point being proved), but the death of Christ is referred to. And John uses the term 'blood' because it is not the dying itself which is in mind, but the life poured out, of which blood is the symbol. See Lev. 17: 11, 14. Christ's blood of sacrifice pointed to the life he gave for men, and hence bore witness to him as the Possessor and Giver of life. Our life was in the blood. And the Author of life is the Christ. **Not by water only, but by water and blood.** Literally, *Not in* (ἐν) *the water only, but in the water and in the blood.* The article 'the' and preposition 'in' are prefixed to 'water' and 'blood' in each case, and point out the objects as those named before; also as weighty and significant; and as they are used with each term, they mark the independence of the water and blood as witnesses. The use of 'in' shows that its objects are now recalled as elements in which, rather than means by which, Christ manifested himself. The general purpose of this part of the verse is to show that Christ is proved by his witnesses to be, not only the life of the world, but such life by death. **And it is the Spirit that beareth witness.** The Spirit, given in connection with Christ's coming, both at Pentecost and as a permanent blessing in the Church, is the most direct witness (John 15: 26) to the same fact that Christ is the Source and Giver of life, and therefore the Son of God. **Because the Spirit is** (*the*) **truth.** Not the symbol (as water, or blood), but the truth itself, directly uttering God's nature; and for that reason a witness to be at once acknowledged, and speaking directly what the others utter indirectly. Before taking up the next verses, observe that all after the words "bear record" (μαρτυροῦντες) in ver. 7, extending to the words "the Spirit" (τὸ πνεῦμα) in ver. 8, should be blotted out of the Epistle. It is found in no New Testament manuscript before the sixteenth century. No determination of modern criticism is more certain than the spurious character of this part of the text. And it seems utterly foreign to the argument John is evolving. We take up the genuine part.

7, 8. For. Reason for citing the Spirit as a witness with the 'water' and the 'blood.' **There are three that bear witness in earth.** They are all viewed as if personal witnesses, taking that character from the leading, interpreting witness, the Holy Spirit. And they are three; the rule for testimony did not require more. (2 Cor. 13: 1.) **The Spirit, and the water, and the blood.** By the repeated connectives and articles, they are made as distinct as possible. The Spirit here leads. His testimony is the more direct and immediate, and takes up into itself that of the other two. **And these** (*the*) **three agree in** (*the*) **one.** The one thing, the one purport. They all bear in one direction, speak to one truth, that Jesus is the Source of life, and hence the Son of God. That life, life, belongs pre-eminently to him, is their one voice, their one evidence. If so, he is the one anointed with the Spirit, who is life; and if thus Anointed, he is the Christ, the Son of God. And the water of baptism, the blood of atonement, and, most directly, the Holy Spirit in his renewing work, are now still speaking of him who is the Life, and asserting his divine nature before us. Must we not believe with the highest faith?

9. If we receive (as we do; 'if' with the indicative) **the witness of men, the wit-**

God is greater: for this is the witness of God which he hath testified of his Son.

10 He that believeth on the Son of God hath the witness in himself: he that believeth not God hath made him a liar: because he believeth not the record that God gave of his Son.

11 And this is the record, that God hath given to us eternal life, and this life is in his Son.

witness of God is this, that he hath borne witness
10 concerning his Son. He that believeth on the Son
of God hath the witness in him: he that believeth
not God hath made him a liar; because he hath not
believed in the witness that God hath borne con-
11 cerning his Son. And the witness is this, that God
gave unto us eternal life, and this life is in his Son.

ness of God (whatever it is) **is greater.** And therefore (argument from the less to the greater) ought even more readily to be received. **For this is the witness of God,** etc. Better, as in the Revised Version: "*For the witness of God is* (pre-eminently) *this.*" In the warmth of writing, John becomes compressed, elliptical. "And why," he silently says, "do I speak of the testimony of God? This is the reason, because this consentient testimony of the water, the blood, and the Spirit, is nothing short of being the testimony of God himself." **Which**—rather, *that* (ὅτι not ἥν, according to ℵ A B and most versions). **He hath** (an admitted and well-known fact) **testified of** (*concerning*) **his Son.** That testimony is still (perfect tense) extant, and calls for the implicit faith of men.

10. He that believeth on (literally, *into;* the faith reaching into and lodging in a personal object) **the Son of God hath the witness in himself.** The testimony of God concerning his Son, that he is his true Son, and the Giver of life. By believing in Christ, this divine testimony becomes a part of one's self, a self-evidencing experience. The believer has a joyful, firm conviction, from which nothing can move him, that Christ is a living reality, the very Fountain of life. He that believes has the testimony in himself; he that believes not, has the testimony, but it is outside of him. The passage before us has been regarded as parallel with Rom. 8: 16. The two passages are alike in this, that they both speak of an inward witness of the Spirit in experience; but they differ in this, that in the one case, the Spirit testifies and assures of our own sonship, while in the other case he testifies and assures of Christ's Sonship. Both passages are, at their root, related to Psalm 25: 14. It is the experimental knowledge of spiritual facts possessed by the regenerate. **He that believeth not** (μὴ, a supposed case) **God** (his word, or testimony) **hath made** (and his abiding unbelief continues to make; perfect tense) **him a liar.** If God were a liar, he could not treat his testimony differently. He who receives not God's testimony made to the reason of all, by the water, the blood, and the Spirit, treats him just as if he could not be believed. And unbelief is a serious responsibility, when it is tantamount to treating God as a liar. John, in his negative putting of the subject, brings out the impressive fact that the unbeliever not only fails of the inward witness of the truth, but positively arraigns the veracity of God. **Because,** etc., introduces a further statement, confirming the appalling truth just uttered. O unbelief, boasting thy rationalism, thou art the most irrational! The least conscious of fault, or sin, thou art the most sinful! Thou puttest thy God with liars, and his gospel with fables! [On the change of negative (to οὐ) in this clause Winer remarks: "In the last words, the apostle passes quickly from the mere conception to the fact; for there were such in reality, and the apostle now brings to mind an actual unbeliever." See § 59, 1.—A. H.]

11. And this is the record (*testimony, witness*). The contents, purport, of the testimony of God, through the water, the blood, and the Spirit. **That** (*namely, that*) **God hath given** (literally, *gave*) **to us eternal life.** The water, pointing to the water of life, the blood signifying the vital principle, the Spirit, who was the very element of life itself, all said, and continue to say, that God gave to us, who believe and when we believed, the true, the eternal, life. "This eternal life is not directly the state of future blessedness, described as already given because it is certain, but the spiritual life in the soul commenced already on earth, and destined to survive the death of the body and be eternal. True believers enter upon the eternal life in this world." (Hackett.) For fuller definition of eternal life, see note on 2: 25. Observe that this life is something '*given*'; in the fullest sense *a grace.* We do not earn it, or deserve it; we only receive it, a pure gift. **And this life is** (abidingly) **in his Son.** We must regard this statement as a part of

12 He that hath the Son hath life; *and* he that hath not the Son of God hath not life.
13 These things have I written unto you that believe on the name of the Son of God; that ye may know that ye have eternal life, and that ye may believe on the name of the Son of God.
14 And this is the confidence that we have in him,

12 He that hath the Son hath the life; he that hath not the Son of God hath not the life.
13 These things have I written unto you, that ye may
know that ye have eternal life, *even* unto you that
14 believe on the name of the Son of God. And this is
the boldness which we have toward him, that, if we

the unfolding or purport of the testimony (μαρτυρία), and co-ordinate in construction with the latter part of the immediately preceding sentence. The water, the blood, and the Spirit declared not only the gift of life, but also that he who came by way of them (ver. 6) had it absolutely and fully in himself. Christ is the eternal vessel of the living water. It is all in him. It is not in angels, or in systems, but in the Son. Only in and through him is life communicated to a lost world. (4: 9; John 10: 10.)

12. If eternal life is conveyed to the world as a deposit in Christ, then the double statement of this verse is the most obvious inference. If Christ and the life are inseparable, we cannot have one without the other. **He that hath the Son hath** (*the*) **life; and he that hath not the Son of God hath not** (*the*) **life.** The Revised Version properly translates the article before 'life': 'Hath not the life.' And yet he has natural life, proving wholly another sort of life to be meant by John. It is only as we touch Christ that we live. Our regeneration is in connection with Christ. (Eph. 2: 10.) To live is Christ (Gal. 2: 20 Phil. 1: 21); and Christ is our life (Col. 3: 4); and we have life more abundantly as we have more of Christ. He who rejects Christ, of necessity cuts himself off from the true life.

13-17. SPIRITUAL CONFIDENCE AND EFFECTUAL PRAYING THE MARK AND PRIVILEGE OF NEW LIFE.

13. These things. Those especially in the preceding section, relating to the fontal life and divine Sonship of Christ, which are wonderfully adapted to deepen the faith and increase the confidence of Christians. **Have I written**—literally, *I wrote.* Aorist. Imagine a pause, or interruption, between the preceding section and the present one, and the tense becomes natural. **Unto you.** The Christian circle, for which John wrote. **That believe on the name of the Son of God.** These words, given in the Common Version, are omitted in the Revised and Bible Union Versions, as they do not belong to the pure text. **That** (ἵνα) **ye may know** (the certainty of the fact) **that ye have** (as a present abiding possession) **eternal life.** What the apostle had just written concerning this life, and its testimony through the water, the blood, and the Spirit, was calculated to deepen and certify this very knowledge. It is the privilege of Christians to 'know' that they have eternal life—are converted, and saved. With many the consciousness is as assured as that of existence itself. Our Epistle attaches much importance to such knowledge. Our present verse indicates a way to this full assurance. We get into life by believing in Christ; but we know that we are in this life by enlarging our view of Christ as the great and only Fountain of our life. To the true Christian the fuller view of the doctrine of life is a means of knowing that he has the life. **And that ye may believe**—literally, *even to you that believe.* Defining 'to you' in the early part of the verse, and showing that believers are the persons whose privilege the writer is setting forth. Awkward as this delayed insertion of the defining clause may seem, nevertheless the critical text compels its approval in place of the 'and that ye may believe' of the Common Version. **On** (*into*, εἰς; see on ver. 10) **the name of the Son of God**—that is, believing Christ, as he is revealed under the name of 'the Son of God.' See John 20: 31.

14. And this is the confidence (or *boldness*). Springing from the sense of union with Christ the life, and from the certain knowledge that we have eternal life. This *boldness*, or 'confidence,' is the same in nature with the boldness spoken of in 2: 28; 3: 21; 4: 17. See Notes. **That we have in** (*towards*) **him.** Towards God, as in 3: 21, where also holy boldness before God and effectual praying are connected, as indeed in Heb. 4: 16. In the full consciousness of spiritual life (ver. 13) there is no feeling of shame or condemnation, and hence the fullest freedom in God's presence. And in that felt freedom there is ready asking. Besides, in this complete spiritual life, God and his will are much in the soul, so that our will in what we ask is

that, if we ask anything according to his will, he heareth us:
15 And if we know that he hear us, whatsoever we ask, we know that we have the petitions that we desired of him.
16 If any man see his brother sin a sin *which is* not unto death, he shall ask, and he shall give him life for

ask any thing according to his will, he heareth us:
15 and if we know that he heareth us whatsoever we ask,
we know that we have the petitions which we have
16 asked of him. If any man see his brother sinning a
sin not unto death, [1] he shall ask, and *God* will give

1 Or, *he shall ask and shall* give him life, even *to them, &c.*

likely to be his will. **That, if we ask anything** (temporal or spiritual, for ourselves or for others) **according to his will** (adjunct of the *asking*, as the Greek shows), **he heareth us**. 'Us' in the genitive suggests that the hearing is with sympathy, and is affected with a moving influence from the Christian or his cause. But what is the relation of this dependent sentence to the boldness before God, just spoken of? The answer may be given by the following paraphrase: "And this is the kind of boldness, the degree of boldness, which, in the full realization of eternal life, we have before God, that if we ask anything," etc. It is that kind of boldness that is accompanied with effectual praying, and is proved by it. It is not exactly confidence that we shall be heard, but a free boldnesss of such a kind that it meets acceptance before God, and makes this acceptance a thing to be expected. Compare once more 3:21; Heb. 4:16. When one is full of spiritual life and filial boldness, his will in praying is likely to be according to God's will, so that his praying is as welcome as his person. When one prays in full union with Christ, it is also Christ praying; it is praying in his name, and the prayer is accepted. (John 15:7, 16.) It is the very will of God. So when the Spirit prays in us, it is the will of God. Evidently a great spiritual life is at the foundation of efficacious prayer. James 5:16 involves the same principle. "To repent a holy name may be an easy thing; but to attain that holy abiding, in which there is such a perfect community of life with our true vine, that it is as impossible for us to ask amiss as for the branch of the fig-tree to put forth the buds and flower of the thorn, this is to reach the very ideal of discipleship." (A. J. Gordon, D. D.)

15. And if we know (as we do, so asking) **that he hear** (*heareth*) **us** (as to) **whatsoever we ask, we know that we have the petitions** (things prayed for) **that we desired of him** (or *have asked from him*). If God gives us favoring audience, he goes further, and gives us our requests. As certain as it is that he hears, so certain is it that he bestows. And note the tenses. We now have what we have asked for. "The perfect reaches through all our past prayers to this moment. All these we have; not one of them is lost. He has heard, he has answered them all. We know that we have them in the truest sense, in possession." (Alford.) The prophetic word of Isa. 65:24 (compare Dan. 9:21) is fulfilled.

16. If any man see his brother sin a sin which is not unto death. The 'any man' is a praying person, a Christian. The 'brother,' according to the analogy of our Epistle, is a brother in the kinship of the new birth. In the case supposed, the intercessor must 'see,' be personally cognizant, of the brother's offense, so as to know its true nature; it is not enough to learn of it through others. And he must see the brother actually *sinning* (present participle) the sin, or in the guilt of it (for one still does a sin till he repents of it). And the sin must not be unto death! it must not be the sin to which death is remedilessly affixed, which hath never forgiveness. What this sin is will be noticed further on. Having spoken of the efficacy of Christian prayer in general, as the proper fruit of the life of God in us, the apostle proceeds to speak of the efficacy in a particular direction—namely, when it takes the form of intercession in behalf of other brethren, others particularly who have lapsed into sin. Here is a priestly office of the Christian, analogous to that of Christ in the Gospel of John, chapter 17. Paul testifies how much he himself bore this fruit of intercession, and be besought the intercession of the churches for himself. Jonathan Edwards begged such help, even from brethren far away. The extraordinary religious interest in Scotland, in 1840, seems to have been begun and sustained largely by mutually intercessory praying among the laborers. **He shall ask.** He is bound to do it, and he will

them that sin not unto death. There is a sin unto
death: I do not say that he shall pray for it.
17 All unrighteousness is sin: and there is a sin not
unto death.

him life for them that sin not unto death. There is
¹a sin unto death: not concerning this do I say that
17 he should make request. All unrighteousness is
sin: and there is ¹a sin not unto death.

1 Or, *sin.*

do it. In this asking (αἰτέω, not ἐρωτάω), as in ver. 14, 15, there is the meaning of beseeching, the most earnest entreaty, as of one who feels his utter dependence. **And he shall give him life.** The intercessor, receiving divine answer, does this—this marvelous thing—does it for the sinning brother. By his intercession he brings to the sinning one the grace of repentance and confession, the blessing of pardon, and the fresh restored manifestation of the Holy Spirit of life. The intercessor is said to give all this, because his petition has caused the blessing to come. The praying man is actually a beneficent force to his erring brother; under God, a fountain of good to him. (That is) **for them that sin not** (μή, subjective, implies a judgment of the intercessor in the matter) **unto death.** Repeats, for sake of preventing mistake, the definition of the party or parties for whom the intercessor's office is effectual, to whom the fresh life may be given. The limit is evidently an important one in John's view. That sin unto death frowns down upon him, denying all hope, and he must except it again and again. **There is a sin unto death.** There is, then, this exception to effectual praying. An important exception, as the repeated notice of the matter shows. What is this sin which results in certain and hopeless death? which is absolutely unto death? It is a sin that John has terribly marked again and again in our Epistle, that of willfully rejecting the testimony of the Holy Spirit as to the true nature and Messiahship of Jesus, the denying of Christ in his true nature. That it is a sin which connects itself with one's treatment of Christ is a fair inference from the doctrine of ver. 12. That it was the particular sin we have pointed out would naturally be suggested to the minds of the readers of the whole Epistle. The unpardonable sin of Matt. 12: 32; Mark 3: 29, 30; Heb. 6: 4, 6; 10: 29, is of the same tenor and character essentially; the doing of despite to the light of the Spirit as to Christ. Finally, if to confess Christ with mouth and heart is salvation unto life (Rom. 10:10), so denial of Christ with mouth and heart, as the antichrists did, must be the sin that is unto remediless death. It denies, and so far as it can do, annihilates the only means of life, and therefore *must* be unto death. And to pray for its remission is to pray for an impossibility: it is to pray against an absolute decree. (Mark 3: 29.) It is to pray for a salvation outside of Christ and the Holy Spirit. In fact, there can be no spirit of prayer in that behalf. [It is noteworthy that John here uses the weaker word, "to ask" (ἐρωτάω), and not the stronger, "to beseech" "claim" (αἰτέω): "I do not say that he should ask" (much less, entreat) "concerning that sin." See Huther on the passage. The Revised Version translates very exactly, following the order of the original text: *Not concerning this do I say that he should make request.*—A. H.] The 'death,' of course, would be understood as the state that is destitute of the new life, which John has so fully marked in the context.

17. All (or, *every*) **unrighteousness is sin.** The apostle is speaking of definite acts, noticeable by the intercessor, and pardonable or unpardonable. Because an offense in not unto death and the person committing it may be prayed for with hope of life, it must not therefore be concluded that it is not properly a sin, violating God's law, and offensive to holy nature. (3:4.) It is a *sin*, though it may be called only *un*righteousness, and therefore needs forgiveness. It is a sin, a grievous sin, whether committed by believer or unbeliever. **And there is a sin not** (οὐ, marking an objective fact, not dependent on any one's judgment) **unto death.** Though it be a sin, a violation of God's holy law, yet it may be one that God can forgive, because it does not do utter despite to the Spirit of Grace, does not deny the very nature of Christ.

18-21. THE SINLESS NATURE, THE HIGH RELATION, THE SPIRITUAL KNOWLEDGE, AND THE DIVINE UNION OF THE CHILDREN OF GOD. THE STANDING OF SUCH A PEOPLE IS INCONSISTENT WITH EVERY KIND OF IDOLATRY.

In this closing portion of his Epistle, the

18 We know that whosoever is born of God sinneth not; but he that is begotten of God keepeth himself, and that wicked one toucheth him not.

18 We know that whosoever is begotten of God sinneth not; but he that was begotten of God keepeth
19 [1]himself, and the evil one toucheth him not. We

1 Some ancient manuscripts read *him*.

apostle briefly resumes or summarizes the chief facts belonging to the new life. The great matter to which he would conduct his readers in all this deep writing is the realization of their union with God in Christ, and the holiness it involves. It is fitting, therefore, that some of the last words of his letter of love and righteousness should touch this cardinal truth of the Christian position.

18 **We know** (as a fact) **that whosoever is born** (or, *begotten*) **of** (ἐκ, *out of*) **God sinneth not.** Does not sin as the law, tendency, ideal, of his regenerate nature. He belongs to the sphere of light. Sinning is not the on-going and ultimate of his nature; but something temporary, to be dropped away in the fulfilling of the new nature. The characterizing, fulfilling, conquering, nature of the Christian is holy as God is holy. For further explanation of this case, see especially notes on 3: 6, 9. The doctrine is inserted again here, not only as a chief and concluding point in the Johannean faith, but to save his readers from inferring that because a brother sins (ver. 16), and needs brotherly intercession, he therefore is under a law and continuous tendency to sin, or his new and ultimate nature is otherwise than perfectly holy and utterly apart from Satan. It is a notable illustration of the complemental and mutually balancing relation of parts of Scripture, to be remembered by interpreter, student, and teacher. **But he that is** (*was*) **begotten of God keepeth himself.** The Revised Version gives not 'himself' but "him" as the critical text requires. And as far as the structure of the sentence is concerned, the most natural reference of 'him' is to God; and the thought is, that the regenerate man keeps God—that is, preserves him in vital union with himself. The new nature holds God in itself, and, beginning in union with him, abides one with him. Here is the true secret and reason of the "perseverance of the saints"; and the assertion of the fact is beyond gainsaying. Alford makes 'him' refer to the man who is begotten again, and, in order to this, construes the first part of the sentence as one of those not unusual cases in which the words do not follow each other in a strictly grammatical order. He forcibly inserts the word *it* (the divine birth pointed at in the preceding verbal expression) before the word "keepeth." [So remarkable is the thought found in this clause by the author that a few words may properly be added. We are sometimes said to apprehend (or lay hold of) God spiritually, and there seems to be as good reason for saying that we retain him in the grasp of our spiritual affection. So Jacob said to the angel of God who wrestled with him, "I will not let thee go, except thou bless me." (Gen. 32: 26.) In so far as manuscripts and early versions are concerned, the weight of evidence (owing especially to the authority of A′ B) is in favor of "*him*," rather than 'himself.' Besides, if the original text was 'himself,' we cannot account for the change to "him"—a far more difficult reading—while a change from the latter to the former would be very likely to occur. Scrivener appears to favor the reading "him" (which is given by Tregelles, Tischendorf, Westcott and Hort, and the Revised Version), but assumes that if "him" is the true reading, "he that was begotten of God" "can be none other than the Only-begotten Son who keepeth the sons of God, agreeably to his own declaration in John 17: 12." Yet he admits that "we have no other example in Scripture or ecclesiastical writers of 'he that was begotten' (ὁ γεννηθείς) being used absolutely for the Divine Son, though the contrast here suggested is somewhat countenanced by that between 'he that sanctifieth' and 'they that are sanctified' in Heb. 2: 11." He might have referred to the Nicene Creed as using almost exactly the form of expression found here—namely, "he that was begotten of the Father" (τὸν ἐκ τοῦ πατρὸς γεννηθέντα) instead of "he that was begotten of God (ὁ γεννηθεὶς ἐκ τοῦ θεοῦ).—A. H.] **And that** (literally, *the*) **wicked one** (Satan, 2: 13; 3: 12. Matt. 13: 19; Luke 8: 12; Eph. 6: 16) **toucheth him not.** 'Him' may refer to God, with the meaning that if Satan does not touch God, he does not touch him who receives God's nature in the new birth; or, it may refer directly to the child of the new birth, who

19 *And* we know that we are of God, and the whole world lieth in wickedness.
20 And we know that the Son of God is come, and hath given us an understanding, that we may know him that is true; and we are in him that is true, *even* in his Son Jesus Christ. This is the true God, and eternal life.

know that we are of God, and the whole world
20 lieth in the evil one. And we know that the Son of
God is come, and hath given us an understanding,
that we know him that is true, and we are in him
that is true, *even* in his Son Jesus Christ. This is

keeps God. Satan, who is the evil one *par eminence*, may tempt and beset and disturb the Christian, but he cannot hurt or even touch him in his vital part. He has no power over the new nature. (John 14: 30.) [The latter view is better than the former, and is somewhat against the reference of 'him' in the preceding clause to God.—A. H.]

19. And is to be omitted. **We know that we are of God.** Born of him, and hence bearing his spiritual nature. A matter of certain and blessed knowledge through previous teaching (4: 4, 6), and through the witnessing Spirit. (Rom. 8: 16.) "Never rest till you can say this," said McCheyne. In this verse the apostle applies to himself and his readers the general truth asserted in the foregoing verse, and sharply contrasts their standing with that of the unregenerate world, so that there is evident progress in the thought, and growth in the strength of it. **And the whole world** (in its natural unregenerate state) **lieth in wickedness** (rather, *the wicked one*). Not merely is touched by the wicked one (ver. 18), but even 'lieth in' the wicked one, in entire union with him; willingly, unresistingly given up to him, completely within his sphere. That the wicked one here is not an abstract principle of evil, but a very person, is indicated by the contrasted personal God, by the unmistakable termination of the nominative form in the preceding verse, by the analogy of John's diction, and by the references adduced under ver. 18.

20. And—(δὲ; here as a concluding, summing up, particle, as in 1 Thess. 5: 23; 2 Thess. 3: 16; Heb. 13: 20) **we know.** The same 'we know' (οἴδαμεν), beginning each of verses 18, 19, 20, gives them "almost the appearance of a confession or summary of faith." (Hackett.) Alford calls them "three solemn maxims." **That the Son of God is come.** Into the world, in the flesh; literally so. Our Epistle has again and again emphasized this cardinal matter, especially against the perversion of the antichrists; and it was a comforting, satisfying fact, at the very basis of atonement and redemption, and the consternation of him (ver. 19) who held the world in his wickedness. **And hath given us an understanding.** This 'understanding' (διάνοια) is "the divinely empowered inner sense," or spiritual faculty, which is given us by Christ, in the effectual action of his Spirit on our minds, making us capable of spiritual knowledge, and in order to (ἵνα) it, as the following clause shows. For the same doctrine, see Eph. 1: 18. The natural man needs this spiritual action upon his understanding that he may know spiritual things. And Christ has come, and has given the Spirit for this creative work. **That** (ἵνα) **we may know** or, as in Revised Version "we know" (the indicative; declaring the object of the understanding and the fact that we already have the object, in one statement) **him that is true** (or *the True One*). The 'True One' is God (John 17: 3), as the pronoun in the expression 'his Son,' that follows, demonstrates. And he is called the True One (ἀληθινόν, and not ἀληθῆ), the real, genuine, God, to assert his distinction from all fictitious or false gods having the world's heart, whether the devil (god of this world) or images. It is, then, one privilege of the gospel to know God; to know him, not merely by the reason or conscience, not merely through theological propositions, but with the knowledge of personal experience, as one knows the odor of flowers, the sweetness of music, or the refreshment of the morning dew, attaining that sensible satisfying appreciation of God, marked in words of Eliphaz, "Acquaint now thyself with him, and be at peace." (Job 22: 21.) **And we are in him that is true** (*the True One*). In union with him; and thus distinguished from those who are in union with the false and 'wicked one.' We not only know God in spiritual experience, but we are in him, in the life element of God the Spirit, in a union of nature with him. **In his Son Jesus Christ.** Yes, in his Son, Jesus Christ. Not even a copulative separates this clause from the preceding

21 Little children, keep yourselves from idols. Amen.

21 the true God, and eternal life. *My* little children, guard yourselves from idols.

one, as if it were so involved in it as to be very nearly a restatement in another form. To be in union with the True One is also to be in union with his Son. The two facts cannot be separated. In fact, we come into union with the Father through union with the Son. (John 14: 6, 20: 17: 23.) This same spiritual union with the Father and the Son stood before the mind at the opening of the Epistle; appropriately it comes out sublimely to view at the close. For it is the ultimatum and glory of the Christian life. In it the river has flowed out into the ocean; the heart is swallowed up in the divine light and love. The new life is filled out when it comes to conscious union with the Father and the Son. **This is the true God, and eternal life.** To whom does the word 'this' refer; to the remote True One, or to his Son, Jesus Christ? With the ancient interpreters, and against many of the modern ones, we must decide for the latter reference. Because, 1. Christ the Son is the nearer and more obvious antecedent, apart from all theologizing. 2. The connection calls for it. John had, in effect, said that to be in the Father was to be in the Son. "How so?" the mind queries. Because Christ himself is the true God, not less than the Father. 3. It does not advance the thought, and seems like a tautology, or repetition, after the Father has been twice designated as the True One, to say, This (true one) is the true God. What object is gained by saying so? 4. Christ is not only the immediate antecedent, but, whatever may be said to the contrary, he is the principal subject of the preceding part of the verse. One has but to read it carefully from the beginning to be convinced of this. 5. Life eternal is the predicate, not of the Father, but of the Son; and especially in the writing of John. See 1: 1, 2; 5: 11, 12, 13. It is the Scripture thought, that the Father hath life, but that the Son is life. To call Christ the life eternal is to unite the closing of the Epistle with its beginning. 6. To call Christ, the Son, the true God harmonizes with statements in both the Gospel and Revelation of John. We may add, that Ebrard, Braune, Schultze, Weiss, Thomasius, and others definitely maintain the view here unfolded.

21. Little children. John takes leave of his readers, and gives them his parting precept, with tender loving address; with a title that reminded them of their relation at once to God and to him, inspired them with Christian confidence, and laid the basis for strong admonition and appeal. **Keep** (*guard*, as in a garrison) **yourselves from** (*the*) **idols.** 'The idols' worshiped by the world round about you, whether spiritual or material in their nature. Separate, guard, yourselves from all the spirit and form of idolatry. The allegiance of your worship and love is due to him who is the True God and Life Eternal, and not to be turned or divided to any object or system of human creation or finiteness. Christ and idolatry are mutually exclusive alternatives in the hearts of men.

INTRODUCTION TO THE SECOND AND THIRD EPISTLES OF JOHN.

I. AUTHOR.

Who wrote these Epistles? No one doubts that they were written by one and the same person. Their form, style, thought, and spirit suggest one author. They have been called twin sisters. But who was the writer? The answers have been somewhat various. Of these, only two are worthy of note: one, that the writer was the person who wrote the First Epistle—namely, John, the apostle; the other, that the writer was John, the presbyter, a Christian disciple, who, it is alleged, lived in Ephesus near the close of the first century. Ebrard sustains the latter opinion; but the weight of critical judgment is for the other view, which is strongly sanctioned by Lücke, DeWette, Huther, Düsterdieck, Lange, Alford, and many others of scarcely less scholarship and acumen.

If in some of the early documents and testimonies these two Epistles are omitted, where the First is cited or named, the reason is to be found in their exceeding brevity, and their merely private destination, rather than in a doubt of their apostolic origin. Irenæus, the disciple of Polycarp, Clement of Alexandria, Dionysius and Alexander of Alexandria, Cyprian, and Eusebius, all give direct or indirect testimony to the authorship by John, the apostle. Even the existence of such a person as John, the presbyter, as distinguished from the Apostle John, is deemed by Alford "very doubtful." The principal reason why the two Epistles have been attributed to any other than John, the apostle, is the writer's announcement of himself in each as the elder, or presbyter. It is the manner of John, as the Fourth Gospel and First Epistle show, to suppress his own name as far as possible. But, writing a personal letter to a personal acquaintance, it was necessary for him to designate himself in some way, which he does, as would be natural to him, with the most modest epithet which he could use, that would be sufficient to identify him. What other term could be so well selected, as that of the elder, or presbyter, to accomplish this, and at the same time satisfy the apostle's modest spirit? For he was an elder, or bishop, in one class with others at Ephesus; and he was *the* elder in being the first among equals in his official relation to the church in Ephesus. And this, therefore, (ὁ πρεσβύτερος, official, not ὁ πρεσβύτης, an old man) would unmistakably designate him. Did not Peter, though an apostle, call himself an elder? (1 Peter 5: 1.) Papias included apostles among those called elders. Another John at Ephesus could not be called *the* elder by way of eminence. The epithet makes for, rather than against, the apostle. The internal evidence of these Epistles, furnished by the style, sentiment, and manner, is strikingly in favor of the authorship of John, the apostle. It is not necessary to make the comparisons illustrating this point.

II. PERSONS ADDRESSED.

To whom were these Epistles written? It is admitted by all that the Third was addressed to a Christian brother bearing the name of Gaius, a brother of prominence, active in behalf of missionaries, benevolent and beloved, but whether the Gaius of Macedonia (Acts 19 : 29), or the Gaius of Corinth (1 Cor. 1 : 14; Rom. 16 : 23), or the Gaius of Derbe (Acts 20 : 4), or neither of them, none can decide. One of this name is mentioned in "The Apostolic Constitution" as Bishop of Pergamos, and some have thought him to be the one addressed by John, but only on the basis of the purest conjecture.

It seems equally plain to us that the Second Epistle was addressed to a prominent and influential Christian sister, Cyria by name, and to her children. Is not this exactly what the letter says, as explicitly as the utterance of the address in the other letter? Yet there have been those, who, fond of remote meanings and fanciful inventions, have understood this Epistle to be addressed to a church, or to all the churches together, under the name and figure of a chosen lady. Some holding Cyria (κύρια) to be an epithet (lady, or mistress), with indeed a literal and not a figurative application, have made all sorts of conjectures as to who the lady was; it even being guessed that she was Martha of Bethany, or again, Mary the mother of Jesus! Those maintaining the figurative application of the term, have even gone so far as to conjecture the particular church addressed. That at Corinth has been named; also that at Philadelphia, and that at Jerusalem. We think we have given the most obvious distinction of the Epistle, and one with which its tenor, and natural interpretation, and the analogy of its twin companion, are most in harmony. Why we regard the term *Cyria* as a name, and not an epithet, and the term *elect* as an epithet, and not a name, will further appear in the commentary.

III. PLACE AND TIME.

The place and time of writing these Epistles need not be discussed at any length. From a passage in the "History" of Eusebius (III. 23), it is inferred that they were written late in the apostle's long life, and their notable similarity suggests that they were written not far apart in matter of time. The journey spoken of in each may have been one and the same. From the suggestions connected with the First Epistle, and from the generally credited tradition respecting John's residence in the last part of his life, there can be little doubt that the place of writing was Ephesus.

The object and contents of these Epistles, together with other peculiarities belonging to them, may be best learned in our exegetical study of them. We only add that the Third Epistle may be fairly designated as pre-eminently the Missionary Epistle of the New Testament. As to missionary enterprise, and our duty to it, it supplies in little space a surprising measure of instruction.

THE SECOND EPISTLE OF JOHN.

THE elder unto the elect lady and her children, whom I love in the truth; and not I only, but also all they that have known the truth;	1 The elder unto the elect [1] lady and her children,

[1] Or, *Cyria*.

1–3. Destination and General Purpose of the Epistle, with a Loving Salutation Within the Sphere of Gospel Truth.

1. The elder. John, the apostle, and writer of the previous Epistle. The existence of a presbyter John, other than the apostle of that name, and living in his time, or a little later, is, perhaps, doubtful; and the attributing of the present writing to him seems as improbable as it is unnecessary. The style, the words, the thoughts, the warnings, are those of him who wrote the First Epistle. The peculiar personal life represented in the one letter is manifest in the other. Every appreciative reader of the New Testament feels the Johannean manner and heart in our Epistle. And then the external and historical evidence on the whole decides for the authorship of the Apostle John. Nor is it foreign to John's way to omit his own name, and identify himself only by some indirect description. No early gospel writer of whom we have any knowledge, would be so likely as John to begin an epistle by leaving out his own name, and calling himself simply the elder, as is done in the present writing. He who called himself indirectly the disciple whom Jesus loved, who withheld his own name in record of the two in John 1: 40 (Godet), who, in his First Epistle, only remotely suggests himself, is just the one to do as the writer of our Epistle has done. The designation "elder," may refer to the writer's general office as one of the elders of the church, or to his matured, and advanced age. The Apostle Peter reckoned himself officially in the class of elders (1 Peter 5: 1); and John may have done the same, assuming the humbler of two rightful titles. In that case, however, he would be more likely to speak of himself as an elder, than as the elder. The latter expression would be more in place if he were to call himself merely the old man. In gospel experience, and in years, he was doubtless the oldest living teacher in the churches at the time when he wrote. How touching and unassuming is the designation, with this reference! The aged servant of Christ, the father in the gospel, writes to a favorite Christian family some words of affection and timely admonition. **Unto the elect lady** (or, *Cyria*). This translation is preferred to that in the Common Version. (Bengel, DeWette, Lücke, Ebrard.) Instances of the ancient use of the original word for Cyria (κυρία) as a proper name, are given by Gruter and Lücke. There are indications that the third letter of John and our letter were written about the same time. If the third was written to an individual by name (Gaius), is not the second likely to be? It is more common for the New Testament writers to mention the person addressed by simple name, than by any descriptive title. To make the translation 'lady,' and then to interpret 'lady' as the church, is a mysticism foreign to sacred epistolary writings. It comes, therefore, to this: that if we have New Testament epistles addressed to brethren, as Timothy, Titus, Philemon, and Gaius, we have likewise one directed to a sister, also by name; and the reasonable prominence of woman in the early church is exemplified. That the term 'elect' is an adjective, and not a proper name (Electa), is suggested by its position without the article in the Greek, as well as by its application also to a sister (ver. 13) of the person addressed. And with what meaning is the term applied to Cyria? To signify her standing in the sovereign grace and eternal choice of God, and her consequent distinction as one delighted in by all within the sphere of gospel truth. In the early Church there was less hesitancy in calling Christians the elect than prevails at present. The old habit might be resumed with profit. God's eternal plan in salvation, and the strength of our standing as

2 For the truth's sake, which dwelleth in us, and
shall be with us for ever.
3 Grace be with you, mercy, *and* peace, from God the

whom I love in truth; and not I only, but also all
2 they that know the truth; for the truth's sake which
3 abideth in us, and it shall be with us forever: Grace,

saints, might then be more fully recognized. **Whom** (that is, both Cyria and her children), **I** (emphatic) **love in truth.** Truth here, and generally in the writing of John, is the truth of Christ considered as exactly conforming to, and representing God's nature. It is the system of the gospel filled with the life of God, and capable of becoming an experience of the heart. Loving in truth, in John's meaning, is loving in the element and sphere of truth so defined. It is loving in truth as a living experience, connecting and bounding both the subject and object of the love. The truth is the bond of sympathy. A love so conditioned was spiritual and holy. A common life of the divine gospel was its ground and reason. Here is the foundation of all abiding Christian affection—not sentiment, not impulse, not worldly beauty, which is evanescent, but the truth of Christ in the soul. **That have known the truth**—have become experimentally acquainted with it; have known it in the heart. Only so can one really know the truth. Then truth and the soul are in vital union. The statement of John is that not only he, but all others who are in sympathy with the truth, and have met Cyria and her children, love them because they discern in them the same truth they themselves have felt, and thus instantly there is a bond of union and affection. It is equivalent to loving in the Lord. Of course, 'all they' must be limited to those who knew the person to whom he was writing.

2. For the truth's sake (or, *on account of the truth*)—that is, to serve and promote it. The truth is the object. What is it that is for this object? Possibly John views his love for this mother and her children as serving the interests of the truth in him and them, and before the eyes of all. Christian love makes room for truth, demonstrates it, and commends it. That which is its basis and principle it also serves as its end. But it is more probable that John has in mind his present writing as that which is for this object. He writes to Cyria and her children with this object before him, that he may serve the truth in them and in all the kingdom of Christ, by recalling precious commands, by warning against deceivers and errorists, and by encouraging them to abide in the doctrine of Christ. What a worthy motive for writing—'for the truth's sake!' What would he not do that this sublime end might be served! How precious was the truth of the gospel to John! He had given himself to it, and now it was his continual study how he might guard and exalt it. **Which dwelleth** (or, *abideth*, ver. 9) **in us.** In John, in the woman and her family, and in all the company of believers. When the truth of Christ comes into union with a soul, it is not for a temporary visit, but to abide there. That soul is its home. And because it is in such abiding relations with the very life of those who welcome it, therefore it was worthy of service, and should have sacred guard. **And shall be with us** (not with unbelievers or the errorists) **for ever**—through this life, and on through the eternal ages, without interruption, without cessation. The truth energized, made alive, in us by the Holy Spirit, abides. It touches the soul as an eternal principle. Christianity experienced in reality continues. But those who have no root wither away. In this verse there seems to be, as Alford has suggested, a reminiscence of forms of expression used in John 14: 16, 17.

3. With you. Not with *you*, though according to text of Lachmann, but with 'us,' as understood by nearly all critics. In the midst (μετά) of us, in our company, along with us, in all times and circumstances. With us, specially John, Cyria, and the children, though not excluding others who know the truth. The blessing is not merely wished, nor is it alone willed, with a certain causativity, as appears in Paul's salutations, but its certain fulfillment is declared; not indeed excluding the wish or the will on John's part, but looking on at once to the sure effect, which has no contingency whatsoever. **Grace**—the favor, benevolence, love of God, considered as in exercise, and actually out-going. "The universal source of all our salvation and new life." (Ebrard.) Trench, in his "Synonyms of the New Testament," too much limits its reference. **Mercy**—the particular exercise of the grace of God towards

Father, and from the Lord Jesus Christ, the Son of the Father, in truth and love.
4 I rejoice greatly that I found of thy children walking in truth, as we have received a commandment from the Father.

mercy, peace shall be with us, from God the Father, and from Jesus Christ the son of the Father, in truth and love.
4 I rejoice greatly that I have found *certain* of thy children walking in truth, even as we received com-

the guilty and miserable, resulting in their salvation. It is a sweet word to such as feel their sins, and realize what they may involve. **Peace**—the full effect of grace and mercy in the soul. It includes the pacification of conscience, the assuagement of fear, the annulling of enmity toward God, and substantial spiritual health and rest. **From God the Father.** The Father, specially in his relation to Christ; yet our Father by our becoming one with Christ. The term 'from' (παρά) here is other than that (ἀπό) uniformly employed by Paul in similar formulas. Meaning *from the presence of*, it dilates the point whence the blessing proceeds, and somewhat detains the imagination upon it. It implies a certain emphasis of the origin of the grace. **And from the Lord** (*the Lord* not genuine) **Jesus Christ.** The preposition (unlike the usage in Paul's salutations) is here repeated to render Christ's personal distinction from the Father more marked, and at the same time to make his complete equality with him, as a source of blessing, more prominent. The term 'Jesus' is meant to express fully the humanity of Jesus. And the whole expression is shaped with reference to current heresies (see ver. 7, 9, 10) as to the person of Christ. **The Son of the Father.** Doctrinal and defensive in relation to gainsayers and seducers. **In truth and love.** The two ground tones of the Epistle, says Alford. The two things to be recalled and impressed in what follows. And they are the sphere and element, the measure and end, of the grace, mercy, and peace declared. The blessing declared shall come into consciousness united with truth and love, and putting honor upon them. The living knowledge of the truth, and the action of love, accompany the blessing. The blessing is of that kind that it cannot be without them. John can announce no blessing which is out of connection with Christ and his system, or which is alien to love. The two terms concentrate into themselves the substance of the fourth chapter in the First Epistle, and impress one that the author of that chapter is the writer here.

4–8. Joy, Exhortation, and Admonition, as to Walking in the Truth of Christ and the Grace of Love.

4. I rejoiced greatly. He had become acquainted with the Christian character of at least a portion of Cyria's children, in some way. Perhaps it was through the reliable report of others; perhaps it was by one or more personal meetings, which could well have happened on some journey, or, still more probably, at the home of their aunt (ver. 13), with whom John was in some near relation. Very likely his acquaintance with the spiritual standing of the children had arisen in both ways. That there had been more than one occasion of learning about the children seems to be implied by the use of the perfect tense which follows. But whenever and as often as he had found out their good walk he rejoiced even exceedingly. The old man was capable of a very lively emotion. **That I have found** introduces the matter of the great joy. The tense seems to imply a repeated discovery of evidence. **Of thy children**—that is, such of them as he had met, or had learned about in any other way. Of the others of the children he says nothing here, certainly nothing against them. Ver. 1 implies well of them all. **Walking in truth.** Holding to the truth of the gospel, and living according to it. The truth manifested itself in their heart experience, and in their general conduct. The truth was the element, motive power, and mould of their life. It includes union with Christ and the Holy Spirit, for these belong to the truth system considered as a living display of the divine nature. So walking, the truth was their theme and confession; it ennobled their looks, it tempered their words, it inspired their zeal; and others might take knowledge of them that they were possessed by it. Their continual testimony, their Christian obedience, their relish of gospel occupations and gospel company, showed to all where they stood. When we witness this, or hear of this, in God's professed children, we cannot help rejoicing, as the apostle did in case of Cyria's faithful children. If

5 And now I beseech thee, lady, not as though I wrote a new commandment unto thee, but that which we had from the beginning, that we love one another.

5 mandment from the Father. And now I beseech
thee, [1]lady, not as though I wrote to thee a new
commandment, but that which we had from the
6 beginning, that we love one another. And this is

[1] Or, *Cyria.*

we are in sympathy with the truth, there are two things that give us peculiar joy: To hear of the conversion of sinners, and to know that those converted are walking, as Christians should, in fidelity to the doctrines and principles of the new life they have received. How a pastor rejoices over the well-doing members of his flock! He knows how John felt. Paul was wont to rejoice much over the persevering Christian faith and walk of members of the various churches. Words expressive of his peculiar satisfaction in this regard are addressed to some at Rome, at Corinth, at Philippi, and at Colosse. Nor is it hard to understand why John and Paul should be so glad over the truth-like walk of those who had professed Christ. In case of Cyria's children, John rejoiced for their sake, for his own sake, for the mother's sake, and, above all, for the sake of Christ and the gospel. And what an opposite feeling of mourning fills our hearts when we find those whom we have known and loved in the gospel failing to walk in the truth as they set out to do. Be sure of this, O Christian professor, that your Christian walk is giving somebody pain or joy. Others are so interested in you, or connected with you, that it cannot be otherwise. **As** (*even as*) **we have received a commandment from the Father.** 'Have' is to be omitted before 'received.' The Father of Christ is meant, and our Father by Christ. The preposition 'from' is the same as in ver. 3; see note there. At what definite past time was the commandment received? No certain answer can be given. Perhaps the time of John's associating with Christ on earth is referred to, and the commandment, of which John has a reminiscence (see also 1 John 2: 7), but no record, is one that came from the Father through the Son. What was the commandment? The connection implies that it was one relating to walking in the truth. Jesus may at some time have given a charge about such walking, in the hearing of John and his fellow disciples, which the gospels have not mentioned. As we have received the Lord Jesus, so we must walk in him. Being a Christian is not only to begin, but to continue in gospel doctrine and life. Nor is it to have something hid in the heart, about which others cannot know anything, but it is to let one's light shine so that others may see and glorify the Father in heaven. The walking is something recognizable. The command to walk in the truth is therefore virtually, first a charge to continue in the Christian way, and second, to give evidence of our new life to others. And so shall joy be awakened around.

5. And now (having made the preliminary statements which the writer wished to make) **I beseech** (or *ask*, not as a beggar, αἰτέω, but as one who has a right to ask, ἐρωτάω) **thee, lady** (*Cyria*), **not as though I wrote** (or *as writing*, for the best text requires the participle) **a new commandment, but that which we had from the beginning** (that is, at first, when Christ was on earth, John 15: 12), **that we** (John puts himself under one law with all Christians) **love one another.** This is the *aim* of John's asking, or entreaty, *that* (ἵνα) we love one another. So Christ's command will be fulfilled. He asks Cyria to do her part in this fulfillment. For the fine purport of this command, the sense in which it is new and the sense in which it is not new, and a defense of its exclusive application to the family of Christ, see notes on 1 John 2: 7, 8; 3: 23; 4: 7. The relation of our verse to the preceding suggests the relation of brotherly love to walking in truth. Thy children walk in truth: And now I beseech thee that we love one another. Truth is the divine principle of Christianity received in union with God. Brotherly love is the outflow, fruit, fulfillment, of that living principle. Having been grafted into God's nature in the new birth, and so receiving the very truth of God, we must love as God loves, and so love all God's children with a peculiar fondness. The truth life is logically prior to love of the brethren, but involves it as its crown and completion. It was this intimate union of the two that led John, having spoken of a walk in the truth, to follow at once with a reminder concerning love. Living truth and

6 And this is love, that we walk after his commandments. This is the commandment, That, as ye have
heard from the beginning, ye should walk in it.
7 For many deceivers are entered into the world,

love, that we should walk after his commandments.
This is the commandment, even as ye heard from the
7 beginning, that ye should walk in it. For many

Christian love imply each other in every renewed soul. There is an instructive hint in John's use of that word 'beseech,' or *ask.* He does not command. God commands; it is our office to entreat and beseech. (2 Cor. 5: 20.) We may not dictate or drive; it is ours to do simply the earnest and subdued work of beseeching. Oh, for the tenderness of John and the tears of Paul in addressing our dying fellow men! Our verse does not declare to Cyria a new duty or doctrine. It is only a reminder of what had been spoken of to her, doubtless, over and over again. Probably scores of times she had heard about it in meetings where she had been present. Of the leading things in our religion we need frequent reminding, and may not shrink from the repetition of important teachings.

6. And this is love. 'This' is the predicate. The love principle is this. That is, this is its action, the direction it takes, its working. See 1 John 5: 3, and compare John 14: 15, 21, 23. **That we walk after his** (the Father's; compare ver. 4) **commandments.** The commands of the gospel made through Christ and the apostles are those here in mind. They relate to the whole circle of Christian obligation and obedience. They imply indeed all the moral law of whatsoever age. They include belief, confession, baptism, and observance of the Lord's Supper. Love clothes itself in these commands. Obedience to all the will of God is its natural outworking and manifestation. So is it made perfect. The new life runs in the channels of God's will. Its native language is: "I will run in the paths of thy commandments." Thus, while walking in truth fulfills itself in love, love fulfills itself in all obedience. And thus the love of John's exhortation is "not an effeminate, self-seeking, self complacent love, but a love which manifests itself in the steady discharge of every obligation." It is no mere emotional or sentimental principle that he has in mind, but a vigorous, practical spring of action, such as that which we see in the Father and was manifest in Jesus Christ. **This is the commandment.** The one commandment in which God's other commandments are summed up. (Alford.) Or, at least a principal command, which has many applications, and covers much of the ground of Christian action. **That, as ye** (Cyria and her children) **have heard from the beginning.** From the time when ye first heard anything about Christianity. **Ye should walk in it.** That is, in love. If 'it' meant the commandment, the preposition governing it would have been "after," or according to, as in former part of the verse. Walking in love is doing the practical deeds of love. The specific deed of love which the apostle intends at this point is the exercise of brotherly love. And this is the argument of the whole verse: Love as a principle, or God's love in the soul, leads to the doing of the commands. A chief command, or the substance of all the commands, is that we should have all our walk in love, that all our acting should be in love, which includes our acting toward our brethren. Therefore, if we have the love of God in us, we shall do God's will as to the particular matter of brotherly love. And so the particular command of ver. 5 is enforced by an argument derived from love inself.

7. For. This introduces a reason why Cyria and her children should adhere steadfastly to the gospel command of love, and continue to walk in love, and why the writer so much urges it. John teaches impressively that one of the best preservatives against being led away into the error of false teachers is to keep one's self in the life of spiritual love. As long as this love abides warm and active in the heart, we are comparatively safe against the snares of doctrinal error. For it is an instinct that follows and distinguishes the truth, as the bee does the honey. John feels that if the persons addressed let their love wax cold and their practical spiritual life shrink up, they would be a ready prey for the errorists who were abroad, many in number, like devouring beasts and wily serpents. "Therefore, by all means," he says, "continue to walk in love." Ecclesiastical history shows that not till the early churches waxed cold in their love, in practical spiritual vitality, did antichrist make effectual inroads upon

who confess not that Jesus Christ is come in the flesh.
This is a deceiver and an antichrist.
8 Look to yourselves, that we lose not those things
which we have wrought, but that we receive a full
reward.

deceivers are gone forth into the world, *even* they
that confess not that Jesus Christ cometh in the
8 flesh. This is the deceiver and the antichrist. Look
to yourselves, that ye [1] lose not the things which
[2] we have wrought, but that ye receive a full reward.

1 Or, *destroy*......2 Many ancient authorities read *ye*.

them, and errors of docetism and sacramentarianism flourish. Deadness of experience was the fatal step towards falsity of doctrine. Materialism, spiritualism, and other forms of religious error, are far more likely to allure adherents from the cold and lifeless members of our churches, than from others. There is indeed another class of Christians who are easily duped by doctrinal extravagances—namely, such as are puffed up with spiritual pride. Yet these are not another class, for as a rule these very ones are, above all, lacking in tender love of the brethren. Spiritual pride is a form of self-love, which excludes the finer emotions of love to all the church. The statement to be emphasized here is that the perversion of one's inner spiritual life exposes one to the power of error. But there was a special reason for adhering to brotherly love, in the form of error which the false teachers were inculcating at the time John wrote. They were teaching that Jesus Christ had not come in the flesh, that he had only the appearance of human nature. This teaching was logically a foe to the existence of brotherly love. For love is received only in union with God. And no man can come into union with God save through the incarnation of his Son. And if Christ be not actually incarnated, then union with God, and consequent spiritual love, are impossible. Wherefore, John says, "Cling to this love, walk in it, as something which the deceivers are undermining by their false doctrine of the person of Christ." In another way still, this deceptive doctrine of Christ was utterly against the exercise of brotherly love—namely, this: We love our brother first in the human nature of Christ. If he had no human nature, if he did not truly become one of us, then we shall be far less likely to love our brethren. "Therefore," would John say, "hold to this matter of Christian love as something which the errorists would certainly cheat you out of, or render impracticable." This whole point illustrates how directly a great error concerning Christ may affect one's religious experience and life, and the unspeakable importance of the Christian guarding himself against the slightest departure from right Christological beliefs. **Many deceivers** (whose work is to make others wander) **are entered** (rather, *are gone forth*, perhaps *from us*, as in 1 John 2: 19) **into the world.** In doing so they became missionaries of error. **Who confess not** (Revised Version, "Even they that confess not") **that Jesus Christ is come** (*cometh*) **in the flesh.** Thus denying the fact and even the possibility of the incarnation. The expression is not used of the second coming of Christ. **This** (*such an one* as just described; οὗτος here nearly equal to τοιοῦτος, as in 1 John 2: 22, "Odes" of Pindar, 4, 38, and possibly Matt. 16: 18) **is a** (*the*) **deceiver and an** (*the*) **antichrist.** The definite article is expressed with both nouns in the Greek. The one talked of and warned against in the primitive teaching, or at least one fulfilling the idea of the antichrist. See on 1 John 2: 18, 22; 4: 3. Here, as before, is evidence that an antichrist is not one who denies outright the Lord Jesus Christ, but one who, professing to receive Christ, yet denies essential things about him. It is one who teaches Christ, yet not *the* Christ in his full nature and office. It is evident, with this definition, that there are many antichrists still in the world.

8. Look to yourselves. *Be on your guard against, beware of, yourselves.* (Phil. 3: 2.) It is possible that Cyria and her children may have been in some peculiar danger, may have just begun to come short, or at least to listen to one of the false charmers. Hence his sudden cry of warning, designed to be as a shock to persons on the very edge of peril. **That we** (rather, *ye*) **lose not those things which** (or, *what*) **we** (rather, *ye*) **have wrought.** That is, in the past for their own salvation (Phil. 2: 12) and for the truth (Gal. 2: 18) among the people. Their own work would be subverted, and its results greatly marred, if not annulled, should they slide into the vortex of the errorists, whose teaching, as truly as that of the Judaists of Galatia, brought in

9 Whosoever trangresseth, and abideth not in the doctrine of Christ, hath not God. He that abideth in	9 Whosoever [1] goeth onward and abideth not in the teaching of Christ, hath not God: he that abideth

[1] Or, taketh the lead.

another gospel. **But that we** (rather, *ye*) **receive a full reward.** A reward that is full. The term 'full' is predicative and emphatic. Their adhesion to the pure truth of the gospel, especially under strong temptation, should bring them the fullest reward of life and joy, beginning in this world, but perfected in the next. Every Christian who reaches heaven will have all the joy he can contain; but the faithful, growing Christian will have a capacity for a far larger life and joy than the unfaithful one, and in that respect enjoy a fuller reward. A man is saved by grace through faith, but he is rewarded at last according to his works. (1 Peter 1: 17; Rom. 2: 6; Rev. 22: 12.) The second person has been given to the verbs of this verse, in accordance with the latest judgments of the original text.

9–13. Doctrinal Error as to Christ Involves Atheism. Treatment to be Rendered to those who Hold the Error of Antichrist. Fullness of John's Heart toward the Absent Family to whom he writes. Greeting from Certain of Cyria's Kindred.

There is a wonderful exhibition of both severity and tenderness in this part of the Epistle; severity toward the errrorists, tenderness toward the truth-loving Christian. A side of John's character is revealed that is sometimes ignored. It is, indeed, the truly tender man who can be severe. The beloved disciple was a son of thunder.

9. Whosoever transgresseth, and abideth not in the doctrine of Christ (the doctrine relating to Christ) **hath not God** (himself). The word 'God' is in the place of emphasis in the Greek. Any radical departure from the true doctrine of Christ's nature is in fact atheism. One cannot theorize against Christ, without theorizing against God. He who rejects Christ rejects the God and Father of Christ. There is a kind of double statement of the errorists' fault in our passage. 'Transgresseth' does not mean here the committing of sin in general, but, in etymological strictness, the idea of going beyond, or going before. See Revised Version. It is here spoken of those who think they have gotten before, or beyond, others in the doctrine of Christ. A doctrinal transgression is meant, a getting beyond the truth, a heady and froward departure from the truth. It seems to be a fit term to apply to those self-confident progressives in all ages, who leave behind the orthodox standards, deeming them outworn. But whosoever gets ahead, and does not abide in the doctrine of Christ, is a false progressive. The doctrine of Christ referred to by John is, as the connection suggests, that which respects his person. The true doctrine was that he was the eternal son of God come in real flesh, the Word made flesh, living as one of us, and having a real human nature as well as very Deity. Such was the Christ who had come to save men. Now, as we learn in the first Epistle as well, a class of professed Christian teachers had arisen, who denied this true doctrine, and claimed that Christ only *appeared* to have a human nature, and hence was in no true sense incarnate. It was a species of teaching which in fact overturned the Christian system, and made spiritual life and love in us impossible. If true, there could be no such thing as an atonement for sin, and no such attainment as union with God, since both these are by the human nature of Christ in mysterious connection with the divine. More than this, those who teach these things have not God. Logically, they are atheists. They deny the God in Christ, revealing himself by Christ, and the Father's true relation to Christ; and they deny the Father's express revelation concerning the person of Christ, thus making him a liar, the same as no God. Nor do those who so pervert the facts of Christ's person, have God in an experimental sense. They dispossess themselves of God practically as well as theoretically. When one departs so far in his theory he is not a Christian. What an illiberal person this John is forsooth! Some of the false teachers referred to were no doubt amiable and morally consistent persons; yet John declares them godless, simply because they departed from the doctrine of Christ. He judged them

the doctrine of Christ, he hath both the Father and the Son.

10 If there come any unto you, and bring not this doctrine, receive him not into *your* house, neither bid him God speed:

11 For he that biddeth him God speed is partaker of his evil deeds.

in the teaching, the same hath both the Father and
10 the Son. If any one cometh unto you, and bringeth
not this teaching, receive him not into *your* house,
11 and give him no greeting: for he that giveth him
greeting partaketh in his evil works.

---

by their views. See on 1 John 2: 23: 5: 12. **He that abideth in the doctrine of Christ.** ('Of Christ' is of course understood from what precedes, though the words are not in the best text.) **He** (see use of οὗτος in ver. 8) **hath both the Father and the Son.** He has the Son just as he is, and he who thus has the Son has the Father also; since the very relation of son implies a father, and the God-nature of the one is the God-nature of the other; and he who has taken the Son as he is has taken the Father's word concerning him, and hence the Father himself. Besides the natural and and spiritual union of Father and Son is such that he who truly has the one has the other. See John 14: 6-9. The following great truths are implied: 1. The incarnation of Christ is the very basis of Christianity. 2. Christ has one divine nature with the Father. 3. Our doctrine does affect our Christian standing. How important John's communication to Cyria in this brief letter!

10. If there come any unto you. Better, as in the Revised Version, *If any one cometh to you.* The mood (indicative) shows that the case is not merely hypothetical. Such persons were sure to come, or indeed had already come. If some had already been entertained by Cyria, this would account for the sharpness of his warning in ver. 8, and make more natural the great directness and emphasis of the order in the present verse. The home of Cyria was evidently a hospitable one, where itinerant ministers were wont to find entertainment. Evangelists and teachers were passing from church to church, and from place to place, probably much more than we now witness. The generous family is warned against receiving to their home such visitors indiscriminately. If one comes bearing the false view of Christ just described, they are not to entertain him. John tells them this with apostolic authority; not with spite towards the deceivers, but in the interest of the precious faith, and of precious friends. He does not forbid an act of humanity to even a false teacher, if perishing with hunger or sickness. The false teacher in question comes not as a mendicant for food and shelter, but as a Christian minister, to receive attention as such; in which case he is not to be admitted to hospitality, for that would be to recognize him as a minister of Christ. The woman's house was a temporary home of traveling Christian ministers. The neighbors, the Church, so understood it. If she had there the false, were they not the same to her as the true? Did she not indorse them? Besides, to receive them would be to give them aid and comfort in their perverse position, and encourage them in feeling that they could corrupt the gospel, and continue all their privileges. What is more, they should not be received, because their coming might vitiate the doctrines of the family. "Evil communications corrupt good manners." (1 Cor. 15: 33.) One cannot touch fire without being burned. In all this warning of John there is plainly implied the duty of separating from all teachers who come under the head of antichrist (see notes on ver. 7), not only in the Church but outside of the Church. This is a "withdrawal" that means something. Compare 1 Cor. 5: 11; also Rom. 16: 17; Gal. 1: 8, 9; 2 Thess. 3: 6, 14; 2 Tim. 3: 5; Titus 3: 10, 11. The apostles require us to be very decided in marking and avoiding those who, assuming to be Christ's servants, are yet destroying the Christian system by deceptive teachings or gravely defective conduct. **Into your house** (literally, *into house*) —a familiar expression.

11. For he that biddeth him God speed (the same word, χαίρειν, which in James 1: 1 is rendered *greeting*, in the Common Version) **is partaker of his evil deeds.** Compare Revised Version. The fellowship of evil deeds, in all their enormity, is thus established between the well-wisher and the evil doer. The force of the statement is obvious, and its argument undoubted. We are to avoid every act, positive or negative, implying community with antichrist. Note that John calls the acts of the errorists 'evil deeds.'

12 Having many things to write unto you, I would not *write* with paper and ink: but I trust to come unto you, and speak face to face, that our joy may be full.

12 Having many things to write unto you, I would not *write them* with paper and ink: but I hope to come unto you, and to speak face to face, that your

Their perversion of the true doctrine of Christ was as really an evil deed as any common immorality. "This command [in ver. 10, 11] has been by some laid to the fiery and zealous spirit of St. John, and it has been said that a true Christian spirit of love teaches us otherwise. But as rightly understood, we see that this is not so. Nor are we at liberty to set aside direct ethical injunctions of the Lord's apostles in this manner. Varieties of individual character may play on the surface of their writings; but in these solemn commands which come up from the depths, we must recognize the power of that one Spirit of truth which moved them all as one. It would have been infinitely better for the Church now, if this command had been observed in all ages by her faithful sons." (Alford.) Let all our people be firm in their attitude of avoidance towards those who, boasting the name of Christians, practically destroy Christ. So doing they may be called illiberal, but they will carry out the earnest injunction of John, and show a jealousy for the truth.

12. Having passed through our apostle's reminders of love and sound doctrine, and his terrible charge as to the errorists, we reach his full-hearted concluding words. **Having many** (emphatic) **things to write to you.** To write, in case he had no plan or hope of soon visiting the family. John was one who in the glow of writing had a perfect crowd of things press into mind, and the ardent man had to exercise a very determined will as to what to omit and when to stop. (John 21: 25; 3 John 13.) **I would not write** (this word understood, but not expressed in the Greek) **with paper and ink.** 'Paper,' the Egyptian papyrus, probably the so-called Augustan or Claudian. This and the 'ink,' commonly made of soot and water, thickened with gum, the writing-reed (3 John 13), probably split, were the New Testament writing materials. (Lücke.) The paper was prepared by gluing together the membranes of the papyrus plant, reed, or flag. Being comparatively cheap, it superseded earlier materials for writing, such as lead plates, stones, and skins of animals. The archæologists tell us that the books of the New Testament were written at first on this preparation. **But I trust** (rather, *hope*) **to come** (γενέσθαι, not ἐλθεῖν) **unto you.** He speaks with caution. He does not know certainly that the way will be open for him to go. But he trusts it will be. He is making plans for this. He submits, however, to the wider plans of God. The inspiration of the apostles applied to the truth in hand which they were communicating. It did not imply infinite knowledge. About the general affairs of life, and movements before them, they seem to have had the same uncertainty which we have (Acts 20: 22), and they were not safe against mistakes in common actions. (Gal. 2: 11-14, and possibly Acts 21: 26.) Whether John's hope of visiting the house of Cyria was fulfilled or not, we have no means of knowing. Probably it was. **And to speak face to face.** (Literally, *mouth to mouth*, not an English idiom.) While the old apostle writes to the beloved family, his heart warms, and a crowd of things come into his mind of which he would speak for their instruction and joy; so many, and of such a kind, that he cannot do justice to them with pen and paper. He must wait and write them on their hearts with the living tongue, when he can help his expression by the tones of his voice, the changes of his countenance, his look into their eyes, and their own interposed questions as they should talk "mouth to mouth." We would like to have some of those many things that he would speak to them. But we must conclude that his feeling that for the rest writing was inadequate, and he must wait for the hour of personal interview, was altogether providential. He had written all that it was best to write to the family at present, all that it was best to have come down to us in the letter. For the Spirit who inspired John foresaw that it was to be for us as well as for those near in time and place. The Spirit ordered that this writer should close just where he did. In the New Testament there is neither too much nor too little for our highest discipline, howbeit a thousand things are left there unsaid about which we have curiosity. The wisdom of God is as truly exercised in the omissions and silences of Scripture as in the

13 The children of thy elect sister greet thee. Amen.

13 joy may be made full. The children of thine elect sister salute thee.

things said. **That our** (whether this should be 'our' or *your*, the authority is about equally balanced) **joy may be full.** Filled up, made utterly complete. See 1 John 1: 4, and notes thereon. The cause of the joy in the present case will be both the personal presence of the apostle (Bengel), and the full communication of the truth in oral discourse (Braune.) Personal meeting would be an occasion of mutual refreshment and joy. (Rom. 1: 12; 15: 32.) And then the ministry of the word of life, in such fullness and power as would come of a personal visit, would stimulate the family's joy to the highest pitch. To promote Christian joy is of itself a worthy end of a gospel ministry (2 Cor. 1: 24), and must not be lost sight of in the proportional division of the word to the people, and in the meetings of the church. In the word of truth and in the communion of saints are the highest conditions of spiritual joy.

13. The children of thy elect sister ('elect' is emphatic) **greet** (*salute*) **thee.** On the meaning of this epithet, and the inference from its use in case of more than one person in the same letter, see on ver. 1. It was customary for the apostles, in writing to individuals or churches, to communicate the loving greetings of fellow-Christians who might be at hand when they were writing. We judge that it was a common thing for the early Christians to send salutations to their absent brethren and sisters. The closing chapter of the Epistle to the Romans affords a remarkable instance. In such salutations, both in their source and destination, there is an individualizing of Christians, and a marking of their personal prominence in Christ. Christianity honors and brings out the individual. Compare John 10: 3. The present salutation was for Cyria in particular; and it came from the children of her own sister, both according to the flesh, and in Christ. These children seem to have been near John, in his very society. Very likely John was stopping with them when he wrote. It is supposed that the sister herself was dead; or she may have been living away at the time. But the Christian children remembered their Christian aunt, and sent her their greeting with John's message. This greeting, like all the salutations which traveled from one Christian to another in those primitive times, was more than a formality, more than a good wish. It was an assurance of continued spiritual fellowship; it was a greeting in recognition of a common union in the Lord. A spiritual emotion went out with it to the party saluted, such as can arise in one regenerate heart towards another that abides faithful. It was a motion of the Spirit from one heart to another, strengthening the bond of fellowship and increasing Christian joy. It was one of God's beautiful ministries of brotherly love. The **amen** of the old Received Text and the Common Version, should undoubtedly be omitted.

THE THIRD EPISTLE OF JOHN.

THE elder unto the well beloved Gaius, whom I love in the truth.

1 The elder unto Gaius the beloved, whom I love in truth.

1-4. THE WRITER'S AFFECTIONATE ADDRESS TO GAIUS; HIS GOOD WISHES FOR HIM, AND HIS JOY IN REFERENCE TO HIM.

1. The elder. See on 2 John 1. The writer identifies himself by an ordinary, not an extraordinary, title, by which, apparently, he was particularly well known, and long known; and hence the article. John was an apostle, selected by Jesus when on earth. But he does not choose to mention the honor or authority derived from that office. It was particularly necessary for Paul, in his epistles, to assert his apostleship, because, having been appointed thereto after Christ had withdrawn to heaven, his title to the office was often denied by unfriendly parties. The title, or heading, which ascribes our Epistle to John, and makes it the third in order, is found in some of the oldest manuscripts, as indeed are those of the First and Second Epistles, and is a testimony of much weight as to its supposed origin. There is an air of authority, a supervising interest, and a certain absoluteness in the teaching of our Epistle, as well as in that of the preceding one, which most powerfully suggests an apostolic, rather than *merely* presbyterial, origin. Can we imagine any one short of an apostle saying such words as we find in ver. 10 and 12 of our Epistle, and in ver. 7 and 10 of the second? And then the manner, the peculiar thinking, the theological conception, the spirit, of John the apostle, impress themselves upon us almost everywhere in these Epistles. **To** (writing to, making address to) **Gaius.** Same as the Latin *Caius*. Where he lived we do not know, probably in Asia Minor, away from Ephesus, and on a thoroughfare naturally taken by missionaries going to remote parts. (Ver. 6.) He was a man of prominence, able not only to entertain, but to help on their way, traveling evangelists. There was a Gaius of Corinth (1 Cor. 1: 14), whom Paul baptized, and who was pre-eminently hospitable. (Rom. 16: 23.) There was a Gaius of Macedonia (Acts 19: 29), a missionary companion of Paul. There was a Gaius of Derbe (Acts 20: 4), who went with Paul and Timothy on at least one of their evangelizing visits. It is the conjecture of several that this latter was the one addressed by John. Ver. 4 makes this somewhat doubtful. Besides, there was a long space of years between Paul's era and the time at which John is writing. The name was one of the commonest. (Alford.) One of the names is given in the "Apostolic Constitutions" as Bishop of Pergamos. **The well beloved.** A strong and most enviable distinguishing title, marking a character by which he was generally and cordially known. The term is not a passive participle, but an adjective denoting a quality, characteristic, or activity of that to which it is applied. (Kühner § 234, 1, i.; Winer § 16, 3, 4th ed.) It means *lovely, loveable;* and hence beloved by all those sympathizing in his Christian traits. He was a lovely Christian. Grace had exercised a softening, refining influence upon him. He was forbearing and benevolent; he was spiritually minded and peaceful. His face was a benediction; his voice chastened and assuring. He drew to himself the tender regard of his brethren, and was a delight to Christ. **Whom I** (emphatic) **love.** Loved in general, John loved him in particular. Nor is he afraid to tell him so. **In the truth.** Not truly, but in the truth-element, in truth as a living system or principle, reflecting and involving the divine nature. The words express the nature, ground, and sphere of John's love to Gaius. It is not an earthly love, having a temporary inspiration or reason. The truth of God had become a living element of the soul, both in Gaius and in John. John loved Gaius because he discerned in him, in a marked degree, the true life of Christ which he realized in himself. He felt a union with him in the new life. There was between them a common experience of God. This was love in the heavenly sense, and without end. What a lesson in the understanding of

2 Beloved, I wish above all things that thou mayest
prosper and be in health, even as thy soul prospereth.
3 For I rejoiced greatly, when the brethren came and
testified of the truth that is in thee, even as thou
walkest in the truth.

2 Beloved, I pray that in all things thou mayest
prosper and be in health, even as thy soul prosper-
3 eth. For I [1] rejoiced greatly, when brethren came
and bare witness unto thy truth, even as thou walk-

[1] *Or, rejoice greatly when brethren come and bear witness.*

brotherly love! In the conception of John, love, truth, and life appear to be a kind of trinity, each in all, and all in each, and together forming the unity of the light (1 John 1:5) of God, into which we enter in regeneration.

2. Beloved. John's soul clings to Gaius, and he cannot let go the epithet. The idea it represents grows vivid as he writes. **I wish above all things that** (better, *I pray that in all things*, Revised Version) **thou mayest prosper** (recognizing an agency in the prosperity above that of Gaius himself), **and be in health.** In literal bodily health. The phrase 'in' (or *concerning*) "all things" (not "above all things," which would seem to elevate the temporal above the spiritual) probably belongs exclusively to the first verb. Some have thought that because John prays for the health of Gaius, the latter must have been sick at the time this letter was written. There is no need of supposing this. It is as fitting to desire the good health of a well person as that of a sick person. John knew that the Christian is liable to bodily sicknesses, and he wishes that his brother beloved may be exempt from them as far as possible. Sickness may be sanctified to us; but sound health is a good in itself, for which—as for general temporal prosperity—it is right to pray. In sound health we have more personal comfort, and can accomplish more. It is not an unimportant fact that Christianity authorizes us to desire for one another not only temporal prosperity in general, but good physical health in particular. **Even as thy soul prospereth.** In the same relative measure. John knows from the most satisfactory testimony (ver. 3) that the soul of Gaius is prospering, that he is spiritually sound in condition and experience, and he prays that his temporal life may be equally prosperous, in an equally sound condition. The soul prosperity of the Christian is made the measure of his other prosperity. Has any one a right to expect more? But, alas! what, upon this measure, would be the outward prosperity of the sinner, whose spiritual condition is well described in Isa. 1: 5, 6? And of many professed Christians it might be said that if the prayer of John were made for them, according to the standard in the case of Gaius, they would have only sickness and misfortune. Perhaps not many would willingly consent to have their health and worldly success measured in this way. There seems to have been a gauging of the health of some in the Corinthian Church to this standard, as a matter of judgment. (1 Cor. 11:30.) But Gaius could not suffer by this measure.

3. For (γὰρ=γὲ ἄρα, the causal demonstrative, while ὅτι is the causal relative; its retention in the text is demanded by both internal and external evidence) introduces confirmation of the statement of the soul prosperity of Gaius. The confirmation lies not in his joy, but in the testimony of visiting brethren, and on account of this he rejoices; and he puts joy and testimony all together in one heart-full utterance. **I rejoiced greatly.** See 2 John 4. He is intensely emotional down to old age, and we love him for it. **When the brethren came** ('the' before 'brethren' is not in the Greek text). They came at successive times, and probably more than one set of them, thus making the testimony very ample. **And testified of the truth** (literally, *unto thy truth*, Revised Version) **that is in thee.** The truth belonging to, and distinguishing thee. The brethren were doubtless evangelists, or missionaries. Compare ver. 5-8. It is a simple term which Paul is pleased often to apply to such workers. (1 Cor. 16:12; 2 Cor. 9:3; 11:9; Gal. 1:2, etc.) The truth which belonged to Gaius, and was so amply witnessed, was the gospel of the Son of God vitalized in personal experience and made a part of him. This truth is a reflection, or eflux, of the divine nature, and he who receives it will not only be sound in belief, but will have a soul conforming to God. The truth is in him, not as a mere abstraction, not as a mere creed, but as a life of God. **Even as thou walkest in the truth.** 'In truth' (not *the* truth) is not truly, but in the truth element or sphere. The brethren had evidence that the truth was in Gaius from the

4 I have no greater joy than to hear that my children walk in truth.
5 Beloved, thou doest faithfully whatsoever thou doest to the brethren, and to strangers;

4 est in truth. Greater joy have I none than [1] this, to hear of my children walking in the truth.
5 Beloved, thou doest a faithful work in whatsoever

[1] Or, *these things, that I may hear.*

way he walked in it, from his daily life, from his deeds of love. (2 John 4: 5.) "Ye shall know them by their fruits." (Matt. 7: 16.) The action of Gaius was that of one who knew and felt the truth in his heart. He uttered the views, he illustrated the obedience, he showed the charity, of a man created anew in Christ. These things were manifested spontaneously, as if connected with a life within. So that the fact of this life was impressed upon others. Men went away from him, not in doubt or suspense about his spiritual standing and attainments. They were even constrained to speak of the case. They bore a glad report of it to John. And John, on his part, was made to rejoice exceedingly on account of it. How enviable was the Christian position of Gaius! How high the commendation he received! What better thing could be said of him? He was a man in whom the divine truth lived, a tangible proof of Christianity, a convincing evidence that the life of God, through Christ, had come to men! He who once was a dark, lost sinner was now a shining light. Men took knowledge of him that he had been with Jesus and learned of him.

4. I have no greater joy, etc. 'Greater' in the Greek is the comparative of a comparative, such as is sometimes formed "for the sake of emphasis." (Buttmann.) The best authorized text may be translated nearly literally: *Greater joy have I none than these things.* This distributes the emphasis according to the expressive Greek, and correctly locates the negative, with no loss to the style. **To hear that,** etc. (ἵνα, explicative, says Alford, as constantly in John after the demonstrative pronoun; introducing, says Lightfoot, the clause which describes the purport of the pronoun; but in the older classical Greek always denoting motive or design). Literally, *that I hear of my children walking in truth.* **Walk** (continuously, habitually) **in truth,** Revised Version "in the truth." Here John justifies his exceeding joy in Gaius' case, and tells what his habit of feeling was with regard to *all* his well-doing children, as well as Gaius. It is implied that Gaius was one of his children, explaining his peculiar interest in him. It shows the wideness of John's personal interest, in that it extended to many besides Gaius. The deepest meaning of 'children' requires that those referred to be persons converted through the agency of John. (1 Cor. 4: 15; 1 Tim. 1: 2; Philem. 10.) Yet, as an old man and a kind of chief pastor, he doubtless reckoned as his children all the Christians in that region. He felt an interest and love for them, as a father for his children. This, in part, made him joyful to hear good things about them. He specifies the good in them that above all else made him glad: their walking in the truth as the element of their spiritual being, the bound of all their living; the patent fact that they both led the life and honored the doctrines of the truth. While others about them might fall into grievous sin or error, they were steadfast in the truth. Others (2 John 7) might deny the incarnation of Christ, with the involved facts of atonement and our union with God, but they remained true. Others might violate the law of brotherly love, yet they were faithful. This would give the apostle unspeakable delight. 'I have no greater joy,' he said. For he therein saw his Master honored, his own ministry not in vain, his own spiritual children having the greatest good, and, in place of being a stumbling block in the way of the gospel, giving stimulus to other Christians and affording the best evidence that the gospel is true. Such walking produces joy in God himself, in the angels, and in all shepherds of the flock on earth. But if there be such joy in us over those near to us who walk in the truth, what must be the pain when dear ones turn aside from the truth in doctrine or life? There is no greater pain than this. How cruel are they who thus pierce and crush the hearts of any who are watching solicitously for their souls!

5-8. COMMENDATION OF GAIUS FOR HIS KINDNESS TO MISSIONARY BRETHREN.

5. Beloved. The lovely character of Gaius is still before him; his heart still glows with love towards him. This is the third time, in the course of five verses, that John has ap-

6 Which have borne witness of thy charity before
the church: whom if thou bring forward on their
journey after a godly sort, thou shalt do well:

thou doest toward them that are brethren and stran-
6 gers withal; who bear witness to thy love before
the church: whom thou wilt do well to set forward

plied this term to Gaius; besides a direct assertion that he loved him. The intensity of his affection is most marked. And the basis, the common condition, in both the lover and the loved, is purely spiritual. **Thou doest faithfully whatsoever thou doest to the brethren and to strangers.** The Revised Version translates, "Thou doest a faithful work"—that is, a work worthy of faithful men and men of faith, faithful to the claims of the case, and done in a faithful spirit. 'In whatsoever thou doest (the aorist tense shows that a real past work is in mind) to the brethren and to strangers.' The Revised Version renders this "Toward them that are brethren and strangers withal." The Bible Union Version reads, "To the brethren and that to strangers." The idea is that they were brethren and at the same time strangers to Gaius. Brethren they were who had been on a missionary expedition in regions beyond where Gaius lived. John had dispatched some evangelists to a somewhat remote field. On their way, they call upon the church of which Gaius is a member, bearing with them a letter to the church from John. The church, through the influence of a prominent ambitious member, or probably officer, declines to receive the letter or the brethren. But Gaius, on his own individual responsibility, takes them to his home, cares for them, and forwards them on their gospel journey in a manner worthy of their calling as messengers of God. 'Strangers' to Gaius, they yet had come indorsed and commended by John, were on a blessed mission, were brethren in the Lord, and no man or company could hinder him from treating them accordingly. He gave them his confidence, his love, his home, and his help. This was, in the largest sense, Christian hospitality. For this John commends him, as he had before commended him for his truth and walk. What is hospitality as enjoined in the New Testament? It is kindness to strangers, especially those who are Christians. It is showing them first a loving spirit, and then, if needful, affording them service and help. It is something which the apostles have often brought to our attention. (Rom. 12: 13; Heb. 13: 2; 1 Peter 4: 9, 10.) In the Epistles to Timothy and Titus, it is laid down among the qualifications of an elder that he should be "given to hospitality." (1 Tim. 3: 2; Titus 1: 8.) But the passages just cited show that this gospel grace and duty should be by no means limited to the elders. It is required of all. Even the poor man, though he has no "prophet's chamber." can manifest the hospitable spirit. The coming of a Christian stranger has brought a benediction to one's home and heart. See 1 Kings 17: 8-24; 2 Kings 4: 8-37; 8: 1-6; compare 2 Sam. 6: 10, 11. A genuine hospitality is one of the most beautiful and gainful duties to God's children. Gaius was blessed for his deed, by John's approval at least. Be kind to God's children because they are his. You will be blessed in your souls, and, very likely, in basket and store. "With what measure ye mete, it shall be measured to you again." (Matt. 7: 2.) "Good measure, pressed down, and shaken together, and running over, shall men give into your bosom." (Luke 6: 38.) He that giveth a cup of cold water to a disciple, in the name of a disciple, shall not lose his reward. (Matt. 10: 42; Mark 9: 41.) "Inasmuch," said Jesus, "as ye have done it unto one of the least of these my brethren, ye have done it unto me." (Matt. 25: 40.) Any kindness we do to a Christian, is regarded by Christ as done to himself.

6. Which (or, *who*—namely, the stranger-brethren having returned to John) **have borne witness** (literally, *bore witness*) **of thy charity** (or, *love*) **before the church**—akin to our expression, "in church," or "in meeting." It is the church where John was living when he wrote this letter. The 'charity,' or *love*, referred to is that manifested in Gaius' hospitality. That hospitality was Christian love in action, and one of the best exhibitions of it. It seems to have been an established custom for the missionaries going out from any church to return to it in due time, and report their experience while absent in their work. Thus Paul and Barnabas returned to the church in Antioch, whence they had gone forth, and reported all that the Lord had done with them. So apparently did the brethren of our Epistle, and in their narrative declared

7 Because that for his name's sake they went forth, taking nothing of the Gentiles.
8 We therefore ought to receive such, that we might be fellow helpers to the truth.

7 on their journey worthily of God: because that for
the sake of the Name they went forth, taking noth-
8 ing of the Gentiles. We therefore ought to welcome
such, that we may be fellow-workers for the truth.

their experience at the hands of Gaius. It was good for the whole assembled church to hear the story of such love. They would thank God on this behalf and be stimulated by the example. **Whom if thou,** etc. Better, "*whom thou wilt do well to set forward on their journey worthily of God.*" (Revised Version.) Having sent them forward on their mission in a manner which they are worthy of as God's messengers, Gaius had been the more carful to supply them for their journey, and do them honor as they departed, because of the nature of their mission and the Being they were serving. He treated the ambassadors royally for the sake of the King who sent them. And so the action toward the brethren became piety, and a divine honor. To send them forward in such a manner was well-doing, an act of beauty (καλῶς). It had been so in the present case. It would and will be so in all like cases. So much is expressed by the combination of the future and the aorist tenses of the verbs in the text. Having sent them forward thus, thou wilt do well, whether then, or whenever done. The future states here a permanent fact, or principle. Alford says: "It will then, and not till then, be a good act, when it is done."

7. Because that for his name's sake (rather, "*for the sake of the name*") **they went forth.** The language of this verse is introduced to strengthen the statement that it was well-doing to help forward the brethren, and to develop the supreme motive of the kindness shown. The assisted brethren were in the service of a certain 'Name,' and they were not to receive anything of the people to whom they were going. The latter consideration made the act of Gaius necessary; the former made it a gladness, and a glory. The 'Name' is that of Jesus Christ. (Acts 5: 41; 9: 16; 15: 26; Rom. 1: 5.) It was in behalf of this Name, to proclaim it and the salvation which it represented, to exalt it in the eyes of men, and, if need be, to die for it, that all the early preachers of the gospel went forth. It was that Name that summarized the gospel, called a world to repent, and thrilled believers as with a note from heaven. It was the inspiration of the great movement, and supplied the highest motive to all manner of co-operation. **Taking nothing** (the word, μηδέν, implies not merely a matter of fact, but a principle on the part of the evangelists themselves) **from the heathen.** It was their plan to receive nothing for themselves from the heathen whom they would evangelize. Hence their support must come from other sources, especially from churches already established, or from friends in them such as Gaius was. And so the deed, recalled in ver. 6, was good. The case appears to teach that missionaries going to evangelize a heathen people should go with their support already provided for. This justifies an essential policy of the modern missionary movement, and indicates the claim resting upon the settled churches to aid in the support of missionaries abroad. In the story of Gaius, let the churches read both their duty and privilege in relation to the missionary cause. Our Epistle may be called the missionary epistle. It brings before us a band of laborers going to the heathen, the Name they go to proclaim or to die for, and the source whence their support should be derived.

8. We therefore (in contrast to the heathen) **ought to receive** (*to undertake for, to support*) **such.** Not only the particular brethren sent forward by Gaius, but others serving the same Name abroad, and in similar need. **That we might** (may) **be** (literally, *become*) **fellow-helpers to the truth.** The Revised Version reads, "fellow-workers with the truth," but the meaning is probably "fellow-workers for the truth," as in the Bible Union Version. Those who receive well the preacher or missionary, and further him in his work, are co-workers with him in spreading abroad the gospel of God. The kind helper of the preacher is in one sense a preacher. The supporter of the missionary of the cross is himself a missionary. He who goes and he who sends are one in the work of the Great Commission. We see in Gaius the beautiful example of one who fully sympathized with the work of the gospel. It was his love of the gospel that made him so kind to its servants,

9 I wrote unto the church: but Diotrephes, who loveth to have the preeminence among them, receiveth us not.

10 Wherefore, if I come, I will remember his deeds which he doeth, prating against us with malicious words: and not content therewith, neither doth he

9 I wrote somewhat unto the church: but Diotrephes, who loveth to have the preeminence among
10 them, receiveth us not. Therefore, if I come, I
will bring to remembrance his works which he
doeth, prating against us with wicked words: and

so ready to further them on their way. His deed was done as if to Christ, and he was regarded as if a bearer of the truth to the ends of the earth.

9-14. Diotrephes Characterized, Blamed, Threatened. His Case Made the Occasion of Exhortation to Gaius. Demetrius Commended. A Cheerful Close of the Epistle.

9. I wrote (the best text reads, *somewhat*) **unto the church.** The church in the place where Gaius lived, and of which he was a member. The connection suggests that the 'somewhat' (τι) in the letter was concerning the missionary brethren. Here, then, is a writing of John not preserved. Not all the letters of the apostles are saved in the canon of Scripture, neither were designed to be. There is a suggestion in the letter being sent to the whole church, of a church responsibility toward gospel laborers. **But** (notwithstanding my care to write to the church) **Diotrephes, who loveth to have the pre-eminence among them** (the persons implied in the term 'church') **receiveth us not.** He does not approve. That is the course he takes. He takes it upon himself to say that neither letter nor brethren must be received by the church. And the church is somewhat led by him. 'Us' includes John, as represented by his letter, and the brethren, in whose behalf it was presented.

We come now to the ambitious, arbitrary, pragmatical, jealous, self-seeking, place-hunting, rule-or-ruin, hard-talking man, Diotrephes, the prototype of many another oppressive dictator and willful alien in the Church of Christ. Whether he was a private member, a deacon, a minister, or, as Rothe says, a bishop, we know not. We know that he was in the church, both prominent and influential. His influence and persistency were so great that he was able to control the church. He was able by his sophistry or threats to lead the majority of the church to do a wrong thing. He may have actually succeeded in convincing the church that it ought not to receive either John's letter or the missionaries. He may have excited prejudice (ver. 10) against John and the workers, saying that they were only self-seekers. For it is a Diotrephes that thinks any one who stands in his way wholly selfish and black-hearted. He may have contended that they were troubled with too many missionary brethren, that their hospitality and means were too much taxed by them, that they had as much as they could do at home without aiding any outside work, that John was presuming too much on their liberality, or that he was assuming to control the church too much. In some way, doubtless, the man had been crossed by John, and his ambition keenly wounded; and he was willing to sacrifice church and brethren, in order to gratify his revenge. Possibly we have a hint, in our verse, as to the way in which his selfishness had been stung. I wrote to the church, says John. Diotrephes was not addressed at all. It is likely he had not even been mentioned in the letter; perhaps it had mentioned the name of some far humbler member instead. Diotrephes says within himself: "John shall not ignore me. He shall feel my importance in the church. He shall have a lesson. We will have nothing to do with him or his men." Saying this, he thinks more of himself than of apostolic authority, missionary work, the claims of brotherhood, or the real good of his church. He loves and serves himself supremely. What a contrast between Diotrephes and Gaius!

10. Wherefore, if I come, I will remember (or, *bring to remembrance*) **his deeds which he doeth.** Not only the work which he did in case of the letter and brethren, but the dark habit of the man since. **Prating** (literally, *boiling over*) **against us with malicious** (*wicked*) **words.** Now the apostle speaks with authority. Not with any vindictiveness, but with a God-given spirit of judgment, as Paul in 1 Cor. 5: 3-5, he utters himself concerning the raging devourer in the church. He will uncover this man to the church. Before all, this ambitious accuser shall know that he is known, and the church shall see how it was

himself receive the brethren, and forbiddeth them that would, and casteth *them* out of the church.
11 Beloved, follow not that which is evil, but that which is good. He that doeth good is of God: but he that doeth evil hath not seen God.

not content therewith, neither doth he himself receive the brethren, and them that would he for-
11 biddeth, and casteth *them* out of the church. Beloved, imitate not that which is evil, but that which is good. He that doeth good is of God: he that

led. It appears from the words of this verse thus far, that Diotrephes had been engaged in a series of deeds of opposition, and was still engaged in them. For one thing, he talked, talked, talked; he overflowed, he boiled over, with talk. He would get excited, and run on, to work up hostility, and fulfill his selfish hate. The current of his talk was malicious words against John and the brethren, some of God's best servants. John's Epistle probes his case; what will his coming do? Our verse shows us the work of a possible bad element in the holy Church of Christ. It is the wolf in the fold. **And not content therewith** (not resting content upon these things), **neither doth he himself receive the brethren, and forbiddeth them that would** (or, *and them that would he hindereth*). Instead of saying, as the word 'neither' would lead us to expect, "nor does he permit those that would," he puts it in the stronger positive form, *and those that would he hindereth.* There were, then, well-disposed members in the church. Gaius was one. The man's opposition is not all talk. **And casteth** (the well-disposed and remonstrating ones) **out of the church.** We confess ourselves unable to decide whether the casting out of the church means excommunication, or simply, forcibly shutting them out of the assemblies of the church. It seems hardly possible that it could have been excommunication on so slight a ground. Yet, so it may have been. The ground, in that case, would be alleged insubordination, because, forsooth, in opposition to Diotrephes, they wished to receive and entertain the missionary travelers! Gaius would be cut off by this process. Doubtless, discipline has sometimes taken this mad way when a church has fallen under the sway of passion, and the wild boar (Ps. 80: 13) wastes it. But it is sad work. Apropos to the idea that the casting out is merely from the assembled congregation, Braune remarks: "It might be possible that Diotrephes was wont to hold, or cause to be held, the meetings of the church in his own house, and refused admittance to those who were opposed to him." There was, at any rate, serious difficulty in the church. All was not smooth in even the apostolic churches. There were bad men, and there was bad work, then; and sometimes a perilous crisis came. But the truth, and the servants of the truth, have on the whole prevailed. Christianity has gained in spite of its false professors, and much unfortunate work; and it has proved itself divine. If John came, as he hoped, things were doubtless righted in the oppressed and torn church of Diotrephes and Gaius. And, even without apostolic visitation, many a rent and bleeding church has recovered itself through the vital energy of faith somewhere in it, and has put on strength and beauty; so recuperative is that body which in any of its members holds the life of God.

11. Beloved. The fourth time this glowing epithet has been applied to Gaius in this little Epistle. See on ver. 1, 2, 5. John is about to exhort Gaius, and there is an appeal in the very title he addresses him with. Undoubtedly there was an unspeakable relief in John's mind in turning from the black picture of Diotrephes to a fresh address to one whom he could call his beloved. What enhanced meaning (if possible) it would have to John, from the contrast just dwelt upon! **Follow not** (*imitate not*, as an example, 2 Thess. 3: 7, 9; Heb. 13: 7) **that which is evil.** 'That which is evil,' as shown in the case just treated. John feels so full of abhorrence towards it that he must exhort all, even the good Gaius, against it, against all its influence. "Do not," he says, "in any way catch the spirit of that man's acting. Do not return to him any such spirit as he has shown to you. Be no party to strife, injustice, or severity." **But that which is good.** 'That which is good'; all that is contrary to the work of Diotrephes; all that is illustrated in the examples of the good, such as Demetrius is, who is so commended in the next verse. Continue your kindness to Christ's messengers, your love of the truth, your help in forwarding the gospel in the regions beyond. Follow that which is peaceful and useful. Persevere in all this, notwithstanding your untoward surroundings. Thus even good men need exhortation, else John would not have given it to

12 Demetrius hath good report of all *men*, and of the truth itself: yea, and we *also* bear record; and ye know that our record is true.
13 I had many things to write, but I will not with ink and pen write unto thee:
14 But I trust I shall shortly see thee, and we shall

12 doeth evil hath not seen God. Demetrius hath the witness of all *men*, and of the truth itself: yea, we also bear witness; and thou knowest that our witness is true.
13 I had many things to write unto thee, but I am unwilling to write *them* to thee with ink and pen:
14 but I hope shortly to see thee, and we shall speak

Gaius. The whole shows that to be a good member of the church it is necessary, not only to be sound in the faith, but to do kindly, useful deeds, and preserve in the soul the image of all that is good. (Phil. 4: 8, 9.) **He that doeth good** (as a habit, a life) **is of** (ἐκ) **God.** Is born of God, and partakes of his nature; has come into the sphere of God's light. Your well-doing, your kindness, your Christian helpfulness, proves your alliance with God in spiritual nature. See on 1 John 3: 10; 4: 2, 3. He that manifests the likeness of God is related to him in the new birth. **He that doeth evil hath not seen God.** See on 1 John 2: 3; 3: 6; 4: 8. Not to have seen God here means not to have any opening of the spiritual vision to him, or to be without any spiritual acquaintance with him; hence, utterly without the new birth. It is implied that the evil-doing Diotrephes is in this state, notwithstanding his Christian profession. Thus John assigns his case, and all similar cases, to their proper alternative. He does it in few words.

12. Demetrius. It is remarkable that the peculiar exhortation and character rule of ver. 11 should have upon its one side such an example as Diotrephes, and on the other such an example as Demetrius. With what satisfaction could the writer—taking Gaius in thought with him—turn from the former to the latter! Who is Demetrius? Is he a member of the church where Gaius lived? or is he one whom John sends there to bear the present needed letter and give support to the shattered cause? Not the former, since in that case John would have appealed to the good opinion of Gaius concerning Demetrius. The other view commends itself as reasonable. In sending him John emphasizes his good standing, in order that Gaius may receive him with confidence, and that others may be favorably influenced by his coming. **Hath the good report** (or *witness*) **of all**—that is, of all who know him. He is a man of good report. When 'witness' is used absolutely, as here, it always denotes good testimony. (Acts 6: 3; 10: 22, etc.) **And of the truth itself.** 'Truth' here must have a meaning harmonious with the Johannean view of it, so largely developed in these epistles. It is here the truth of the gospel as a living principle in Demetrius. That truth so manifestly in him testifies to him as to what he is, as Gaius indeed will see when he meets him. **Yea, and we also** (emphatic) **bear witness.** In this letter 'we' is chiefly the apostle himself, with some reminiscence perhaps of apostolic associates, whose voices he knew would be with him could they speak. Compare 1 John 1: 3. *And yet thou* (as the best critical text gives it) **knowest that our witness is true** (ἀληθής, not ἀληθινός). True in quality; true morally; true in the very strongest sense. Such pre-eminently is apostolic testimony, as Gaius knows. A manifestly weighty evidence of the apostolic origin of the letter. It is natural as coming from John the apostle (John 19: 35; 21: 24), but unnatural for another. Happy the Christian brother, who has as good a report as Demetrius had, and whose Christianity shines forth from him as unmistakably!

13. I had many things to write. His heart is full of them. The emergency suggests them. The strong personal attachment to the man addressed calls them up. But he must desist, till he can meet his friend face to face, as he hopes soon to do. Then he can pour out his thoughts, without the limits or restraints of paper and pen, and inscribe them on Gaius' heart with the vividness which personal intercourse, the look of the face, and the tones of the voice are so well fitted to produce. **But I will not with ink and pen write unto thee.** I am unwilling to go on writing more to thee; present tense. See on 2 John 12.

14. We divide ver. 14 of the Common Version, and make a new verse (15) of the latter half, as Scrivener, Tischendorf, Alford, and practically the Bible Union Version, and as obviously required by the contents. **But I trust** (or *hope*) **I shall shortly see thee.**

speak face to face. Peace *be* to thee. *Our* friends salute thee. Greet the friends by name.

face to face. Peace *be* unto thee. The friends salute thee. Salute the friends by name.

He does not presume to say that he certainly shall see Gaius. The certainty of his going is not revealed to him. He remembers that he is an old man, that life at best is precarious, that some unlooked-for providence may intervene to deprive him of the coveted privilege of meeting his friend and caring for the torn and bleeding sheep of the church. See on 2 John 12. **And we shall speak face to face** (or, literally, *mouth to mouth*). As only the most confidential friends can. What a blissful season will there be then! The future indicative here denotes an assurance of hope that the delightful converse will be enjoyed.

15. Peace be to thee. How appropriate the benediction, seeing what troubles and distractions surrounded Gaius, and what anxieties and pains naturally filled his soul! Let the peace of Christ (John 14:27) abide in thy soul; let all health, welfare, blessing (as expressed so strongly by the corresponding Hebrew term, שָׁלוֹם, and not excluded from the Greek term of the apostolic benedictions) come to thee; and let not outward troubles too much disturb thee. The apostolic benediction is more than a good wish; there seems to be something causative about it, conscious to him who pronounces it. **Our** (rather *the*) **friends salute thee.** These are Christian friends (compare John 11: 11; 15: 15; Acts 27: 3), brothers and sisters, abiding near John, who desire to greet Gaius in the Lord, to inspire his courage, and cultivate their spiritual union. **Greet the friends by name**—that is, individually and particularly. The Christian friends with Gaius, abiding faithful, amid the fierce work carried on by the false brother. "Call them each by name, and present our greeting as we would do if present." Christian individuality is highly regarded in the New Testament (compare John 10: 3), as spiritual union is much cultivated.

www.ingramcontent.com/pod-product-compliance
Lightning Source LLC
Chambersburg PA
CBHW021422090426
42742CB00009B/1217

* 9 7 8 3 3 3 7 7 2 9 1 9 6 *